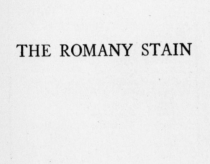

THE ROMANY STAIN

OTHER BOOKS
BY THE SAME AUTHOR

Fiction

PARNASSUS ON WHEELS
THE HAUNTED BOOKSHOP
KATHLEEN
TALES FROM A ROLLTOP DESK
WHERE THE BLUE BEGINS
PANDORA LIFTS THE LID
    (with Don Marquis)
THUNDER ON THE LEFT

Essays

SHANDYGAFF
MINCE PIE
PIPEFULS
PLUM PUDDING
TRAVELS IN PHILADELPHIA
THE POWDER OF SYMPATHY
INWARD HO!
RELIGIO JOURNALISTICI

Poetry

SONGS FOR A LITTLE HOUSE
THE ROCKING HORSE
HIDE AND SEEK
CHIMNEYSMOKE
TRANSLATIONS FROM THE CHINESE
PARSONS' PLEASURE

Plays

ONE ACT PLAYS

THE
ROMANY STAIN

by

CHRISTOPHER MORLEY

Illustrated with pen drawings by
WALTER JACK DUNCAN

GARDEN CITY
NEW YORK
DOUBLEDAY, PAGE & CO.
m. cm. xxvii

TO
HENRY SEIDEL CANBY

TACHE ROMANÉE

Entering the garden after the cool dim stairway it was as if a bomb exploded: heat, brightness, colour, burst open like a soft puff of magic. One of my companions, running up from behind, thrust a wine card under my nose.

Vins Rouges de Bourgogne, I read; and then, among other names, *Tache Romanée*.

The Romany Stain! I thought of white roads in the sun, blackberries in those Suffolk hedges that I most associate with gipsies, bare feet in the hot floury dust. Of water that comes swirling out under the arches of a millrace; of wine drunk in clean hotels at dusk. What is it in the American temper that inevitably concludes that wine means gluttony, that love means lust? The Romany Stain, the dark blood-coloured Eden birth-mark that some carry in their hearts. Forgive me: all I said to my companion was, "What a title that would be for a book."

—Uncollected Writings of JOHN MISTLETOE.

CONTENTS

Contents

[x]

THE ROMANY STAIN

A SEA SHELL IN NORMANDY

YOU first see Mont St. Michel from the toy railway train at St. Jean-le-Thomas. You know then
that what you have always heard was true. After
lunch at Genêts you drive across the sands at low tide,
in a cart pulled by two horses. On a grey afternoon,
with opal storm clouds coiling in the west, the wide
floor of the bay lies wet and bare, shining all silver and
fish-belly colours. The rock of Tombelaine sprawls
like a drowsy mastiff on guard. You feel that if you
stroked the warm granite chine he would rise, stretch-
ing, and fill the empty day with a yawn of thunder.
In all that clean vacancy, framed in the blue scabbard
of Normandy and Brittany, the holy boulder rises, a
pinnacle of stone jewellery. The great ramps are rusted

[1]

with tawny lichen. Tiny gardens niched among the steep zigzags are bright with flowers. With the genuine thrill and tingle of the pilgrim you climb, cricking your neck at the noble sheer of those walls and struts that lean upward and inward to carry the needle of the spire. Pinnacles rally and burn aloft like darts of flame. You can almost feel the whole roundness of earth poise and spin, socketed upon this stony boss of peace. You think of the Woolworth Building. How nice if that too were sown with clumps of pink and yellow blossom and had blankets of green ivy over its giraffe rump.

Your mind travels back to the tough and pious men who carried their stones here and built their little Eden of escape: an Eden so shrewdly scarped that apparently even the 15th century Old Bills of England cursed and withdrew. You imagine the pilgrims of the Middle Ages plodding the sands from Avranches—occasionally losing one or two of the party in a quicksand—and their heavenly exult as they ached at last up the steps of the "Grand Degree" and saw through the dark archway that wide hearth shouting with flame. Yet perhaps mere pilgrims were not allowed to draw near the giant fireplaces of St. Michel? That ruddy warmth that gilded the groins of the pillars, was it reserved for the abbot and the upper clergy? (You saw, I hope, those great columns in the crypt, where the veins of stone rise to their task as smoothly, as alive with lifting strength, as the cords of a horse's haunch.)—One wonders a good deal about the mediæval pilgrim. Was he welcomed and warmed and refreshed, or was he pillaged? Probably the souvenir vendors lay alert for him, as they do

A Sea Shell in Normandy

to-day. And was there a mediæval Veuve Poulard, down by the barbican, with an omelet waiting hot in the pan, a bottle of wine cold in the cellar? At any rate, many a whole ox must have crackled in those vast hooded chimneys of the abbey; and the warrior abbot could throw his bones out of the window on the *goddams*, hustling to get their bombards back to Tombelaine before they were caught by the tide.

So you people this divine old miracle of stone-work, just as you have dreamed beforehand of a still living shrine with candles by the altar, and small shrill choir-boys in scarlet, the flutter of surplice and *soutane*, and dark bells calling across the sandy estuary. Then, as you are taken through in squads by a *gardien*, you realize that this noble sanctuary is dead. It is no longer a church, but a monument, under the care of the Ministry of Fine Arts. The abbey is only a shell: there is not even a chance to pray. The State, with skilful devotion, has saved and repaired the hull; but it is only a hull. There if anywhere, lifted above the quicksands (how often the old abbots must have improved this moral in their discourses), one would be eager to whisper some small silly petition in honour of man's magnificent hopes. But it is not expected. The old fonts are dry, the altars naked, the tall aisles bare as a February forest. The casket of stone filigree is empty. The imprint of the spirit is there, just as those leagues of sand are ripple-patterned by this morning's ebb. But it is only a print, a fossil. The sea has gone out. Even the tiniest parish church, with its Tariff of Marriages (a First-class Marriage 50 francs, a Second-class Mar-

riage 30 francs, a Third-class 20 francs) is in some sense
more inwardly alive. The Mount is not even an island
any more: they've built a *digue* that brings autobuses
and toy trains from Pontorson. It is a shrine, a miracle, a testimonial of man's horror of the world and his
fellows; but its beauty is the beauty of death, purified,
serene, at rest.

You drive away across the luminous mirrors of wet
beach, you see that exquisite profile shift and alter
until it is a scissored peak on sky. You may walk the
ebb sands of the world for ever and not find so lovely
a shell. But it is only a shell, and in its whorls and passages a faintest echo of the sea.

Must it always be so, one thinks, lighting up the pipe
of penitential Scaferlati? Perhaps there is always
something a little dead (I don't defend this figure of
speech, but I like it) about the old masterpieces?
Glorious and terrible, don't they say to us that we are
not to be dismayed by their beauty but to recreate our
own masterpieces for ourselves? The other day I
read Alfred de Musset's gorgeous little fable "Histoire
d'un Merle Blanc": one of those fiery trifles in which
the French genius seems at its most native: under the
guise of tender and naïf simplicity such a clear ember
of satire. My first thought was that de Musset's
adorable little dagger in the heart should have made (if
it had been heeded) so many later books unnecessary.
So far as it bears on literary manners it clicks the latch
to-day as neatly as it did seventy or eighty years ago,
and might have spared us many editorials in the newspapers. I laid it down with the despairing happiness

A Sea Shell in Normandy

that any student feels on reaching the end of a perfect thing: for I could imagine how happy was the Infant of His Century when he finished it. He had reached one of those rare and perfect moments the artist lives for. He had done it, and knew it was good.

Yet it all had to be done again—and has been. And I remembered, Mont St. Michel reinforcing it, that these things must always be done over and over; that there is no durable pause even in the most perfect pinnacles that overlook the sea. Here and there a pilgrim will be bogged in a quicksand, or get caught by the tide. But some will reach, for a one night's reverence, the shrine where the dragon of despair grinds under Michael's heel. They chant their private prayers and penances, they get out the illuminated manuscripts, they sing their sacreds, they make their mirth. They roast an ox in the fireplace, and throw the bones through the window where the critics are haling their heavy bombards through the sand.

SLOW GIN

SANTA CLAUS came back that year even more
tired and discouraged than usual. Mrs. Claus had
a good fire going in the library, his fur slippers warm
on the hearth, but he sat down with a grunt, too
dispirited even to pull off his big boots. But Mrs.
Claus, who knows very well how porcupiny the philan-
thropists and professional genials often are when they
get home, was too wise to seem to notice his depression.
She drew the curtains closer to shut out the sparkling
polar darkness.

"Have you noticed how long the nights are getting?"
she said. "You'll be glad to get back among your
books."

Santa Claus has quite a large library, his shelves
are lined with those fine rag-paper and morocco-bound
de luxe sets of Oscar Wilde and Ridpath and Great

Slow Gin

French Courtesans, numbered (like the hairs of your head) by the Biblioshark Sodality. These are the things that Santa gets stuck with, because no one wants them for Christmas and he has to bring them home with him. Mrs. Claus, however, who doesn't know a 12mo. from an Eskimo, believes them very valuable.

But the old fellow sat staring at the fire in a serene despair, more like Santayana than Santa Claus.

"Well, did you have a good trip?" she said. "How was New York?" (Mrs. Claus is always curious to know about New York. She imagines it as a place of prodigious thrilling gaiety, and Santa has told her about the shop windows and the electric signs, which really are almost as fine as the Aurora Borealis.)

He shook his head pensively.

"The competition's getting too intense," he said. "The bootlegger is the real Santa nowadays in New York. My clients all want the little miracle of liquid flame that evens man with God. I caught a terrible cold going out in a launch to get enough whisky to satisfy my customers. A queer thing happened to me.

"Coming back in the motor boat I fell into conversation with one of the bootleggers. You'd be surprised how philosophic some of those fellows are. Well, somehow or other we got talking about moving pictures, and this chap was saying that the most beautiful thing in the world is the slowed film. He owns a movie theatre somewhere in Brooklyn, but he says he can't afford to show the kind of pictures that he likes best himself because all the crowd wants is the 'Flaming Youth' sort of thing. Well, I agreed with him about

the slowed pictures. I said how wonderful it would be
if we could for a few hours retard life itself just like
that, to have a good look at the astonishing elements of
loveliness that lurk in every movement. Curves, you
know. See things in that leisurely perspective that
God must have. Why even a taxi spinning round a
corner would float like a leaf eddying on warm October
air. But I guess I can't quite explain to you how I
felt about it. I was tired, buzzing about getting things
fixed up for Christmas.

"He looked at me rather queerly. 'It can't be done,'
he said. 'God wouldn't like it. It's *His* prerogative
to see things slowly. But if you can't slow down life,
you can speed up the eye, which gives, relatively, the
same effect.'

"I asked him what he meant.

"'Wood alcohol,' he said, 'has a queer effect on the
optic nerve.' Well, I didn't like his talking like that,
just after he had guaranteed the quality of the stuff
I had got from him for my customers. But, to make it
short, he gave me a little bottle, for myself, of what he
called (I believe) Slow Gin. He said that for a brief
time, and with no harmful effect (physically, anyhow)
it would accelerate my eyes so that life would look like
a slowed film."

He paused. Mrs. C., who knows nothing about
movies, bootleggers, New York—indeed, nothing at
all of life except Ridpath and the Court Memoirs—
was a bit puzzled. But she could see that he wanted
to talk, so she asked a question just to help him along.

"Yes," he said, "it did. I suppose you know—or

maybe, happily, you don't—what a wearisome muscular
exertion is involved in trying to think about abstract
matters. You can feel an actual thrilling and tensile
alertness in the obscure muscles of the cortex. Something the way an electric wire might feel when the light
is turned on. Well, when I had taken this gin all that
feeling was abolished. Thought became perfectly unaware of itself. I saw the movement of civilization
slowed down to its component gestures. Wonderful,
oh wonderful! I think I know now why philosophers
and poets go mad. That's the way they see things.
Do you remember that line of Stevenson's, *'And me-
thought that beauty and terror are only one, not two'?*

"But imagine it," he went on. "I saw the passion,
the momentum of New York in a grave sluggish rhythm,
solemn as a great elegiac ritual. I could see significance
in all the strange wonders that ordinarily flash past us
in a twinkling. Expressions of loveliness and mirth
and embarrassment and anger, that flit over faces and
are gone, these I saw posed and held long enough to be
studied and admired. I saw Time, the sculptor, in the
amazing process of carving Life. I saw the reporter
over the swift chattering keys of his typewriter. I
could see his hand poise and float above the keyboard,
softly balanced as the wing of a gull. You'd have
thought he was writing the most exquisite philosophy
in the world. I could imagine I saw the quick thoughts
of men slowly coiling and rising like heavy smoke. I
saw the crowd of commuters when the train gate opens
at the Long Island Station in the evening. Instead
of that multitudinous pour down the stairway, I could

see the mass gently lip over the top step and descend as softly gradual as cold molasses. I could see the actual face and contour of clownish ecstasies and solitary despairs. I saw two people saying good-bye. Did you ever see that, as it really is?

"The bootlegger was right. It won't do. It won't do to look upon the itemized flow of life. You become aware of the rhythm of it, and it terrorizes you. Everything becomes beauty, and there's nothing more appalling than that. It heats the imagination till it splits like a roasting chestnut. Men are quite right in moving as fast as possible. You've got to go some to get away from yourself. But how lovely they are when they're unaware of themselves! I saw a girl mailing a letter, at that bronze box in the Telephone and Telegraph Building—I always have to attend to that letter box, so many people use it for mailing Christmas cards. You'd have said that she wasn't thinking of anything in particular, but no work of art ever dreamed could be more lovely than the slow stretch of her body as she hovered up on tiptoe to reach the slit. She was so perfect that I could tell she knew she was doomed. You know, that was it. I saw the solemnity that underlies every movement. I saw an audience beginning to laugh at a musical comedy joke. My sensitized eye caught the gradual coming and mounting and breaking of that poor guffaw, like a big wave crumbling in from sea. Phew, that was terrible! Never again. You know how it is in a sleigh. You've got to go fast over thin ice. Well, that's life itself. Thin ice. When you begin to monkey with the Time-sense you turn things either into a hasty farce or else into a Greek frieze."

"I hope you didn't catch a chill," said Mrs. Claus. "I'm going to mix you something hot."

She bustled up, dropped her knitting and creakingly leaned down to retrieve it. Santa watched her with humorous impatient affection. His optic nerves still retained a faint aftermath of the drug, and he was able, as she hastened anxiously toward the pantry, to slow down the image of her moving figure and see it in ponderously retarded tempo. He chuckled. But he remembered the enormous relief with which he had felt his hallucination begin to wear off. Gradually, gradually, he had seen the panorama resume its wonted swiftness, abdicate that lovely swooning dignity, resume its charming absurd hilarities and grotesqueness.

"No," he repeated to himself, "it won't do. Life has got to synchronize itself with the customary adjustment of the mind. And the mind mustn't climb out of the stream and sit on the bank to watch consciousness go by. You mustn't try to split up Time into pieces for all you find is little nasty bits of eternity. Men are determined that life should be amusing, and to be that it's *got* to move fast."

He still thought hungrily of that miracle he had seen: the grave airy dancing of creation, treading softly its dark measure to unheard, undreamed music. He saw again the slow lineament of desire, the leisurely miracle of women's grace, the insane gaiety on frolic faces, the sorry grin of cruelty, the tenderness that returns with dusk.

[11]

Mrs. Claus came with a steaming jug.

"Well," she said cheerily, "I'm glad you had such an interesting time. And what did you decide to give them this year?"

"I wondered a good deal," he said. "I wondered whether to give them another Conrad to teach them pity, or another Anatole France to show them how to mock themselves. But what I did give them was the greatest of all gifts."

He paused and drank down a glassful of hot toddy with a shudder of content.

"I gave them the privilege, for just one day, of not thinking at all."

BAEDEKER FIBBED

"I RESOLVED to renew at Cherbourg the marvels of
Egypt," says the inscription on the statue of Napoleon, where the plump little emperor sits on a horse
whose antic would probably have unseated him in real
life. He does not specifically say which of Egypt's
portents he proposed to revive; though by his gesture
we gather that he means the vast stone breakwater on
which shines the star of Baedeker, guiding pilgrims from
afar. Myself, I was inclined to believe that a certain
Swiss concierge (himself a true Bonaparte in physique)
was a reincarnation of the asp. But nowadays, when
we are more wonted to great engineering projects, the
real astonishment of Cherbourg is the endless caravan
of Americans who flit feverishly through the town without halting to draw breath. The Swiss concierge, in

[13]

his field-marshal's uniform, harries them a little, inflicts a few cicatrices on the right-hand trouser; but most of them escape.

In the summer season the big liners come in from New York two or three a day. Every few hours you see the long strings of railway cars marked ÉTAT lining up along the quay to take the passengers to Paris. Our fellow countrymen come shuffling down the steep gangplank from the tender—perhaps the tender *Nomadic*, or the *Traffic*, or the *Lotharingia*, or the *Welcome*— names so much less imaginative than the *Sir Richard Grenville* at Plymouth. After a brief frenzy in that little blue-and-white-striped shed of the *douane* where the whiskered, cloaked, and sworded *apéritif* officials look so much fiercer than they really are, they climb into the train. At once they fill the restaurant cars and order wine; or you see them sitting patiently in the first-class carriages watching the dusty quay and throwing their money to the ragged urchins who frequent the *gare maritime*. The lovely little town that lies across the basin is hidden from them by the shed. And after all, hasn't Baedeker told them that Cherbourg is "comparatively uninteresting"? So, unless the ship happens to arrive in the evening, they all buzz straight on to Paris. If they land late they go to the Hôtel du Casino, one of those amusing nodes in the great network of travel where sooner or later you inevitably encounter someone you know. There M. Minden, the courteous manager, will greet them with his dark, melancholy, and secretly humorous gaze; and eventually teach them that the first syllable of the town's name is not without significance. Sometimes, coming downstairs toward nine or ten in the evening, you'll find the quiet little lobby suddenly buzzing with a new lot. The *Berengaria* is in, or the *Olympic*, or the *President Harding*. You'll see them sitting in the bar-parlour having a snack before retiring, or looking hopefully for a new copy of the New York *Tribune*. The only French client I ever saw at the Casino was a luckless lady just in from the States who had been abroad so long she had forgotten how to order wine. She came into the bar breathing exultation at her escape from the *régime sec*. Then, as the expectant *garçon* waited for some order expressing the soul and talent of a connoisseuse, her face drooped. She couldn't think of anything . . . and ordered a grenadine—which creates in a French bartender about the same enthusiasm as asking a Liggett soda-twister for a beaker of lukewarm goat's milk.

But by the time you come down to breakfast you'll find that the overnight batch of Americans has already sped onward. Cherbourg has resigned itself to this state of affairs: so much so that if you tell them you intend to stay there awhile they'll hardly believe you, and unless you watch your baggage piece by piece they shove it on the Paris train anyhow. (*Crede experto*.) Those Americans who are still in the hotel when you enter the dining room are perhaps making themselves obnoxious to the head waiter because there aren't any hot breads. As I was sitting happily with my *café complet* I could hear one elderly gentleman crying bitterly, "Hot rolls, hot rolls. I want 'em red hot!" Why do our friends go abroad at all if they expect

everything to be exactly as at home? It is these creatures who account for that deeply submerged glitter
in the manager's eye, and make travel so much more
expensive for the rest of us. At any rate, Cherbourg is
not such a bad place to study one's fellow citizens, for
you see them at a moment of crisis when they are very
keenly conscious of their nationality. With an almost
defiant air they insist on talking English to the em-
ployees as though to prove and ram home the fact that
there really is such a language.

I shall never forget the thrill and charm of that late
arrival. It was one of those long June twilights when
the *Lancastria* dropped anchor inside Napoleon's
Egyptian *digue*. On the tender, anxiously attempting
to gather into one corner his various baggages, paterfamilias was naturally too troubled to have a chance to
enjoy the view of the harbour that lay so lilac in the
evening light; though there was, subconsciously, as
one's eye noticed that long solid line of stone houses
which fronts the sea, the odd realization that foreign
countries are real after all, which quaintly surprises
one anew at every visit. By the time we had got
through the customs, rescuing all our pieces (save one,
containing of course the baby's most urgent affairs)
from being "expedited" to Paris, it was close on eleven
o'clock. The Cherbourg *douaniers* and porters work
like demons at that time of night, "expediting" one to
Paris, for not unnaturally they are anxious to get home
and to bed. And when the boat train, with a wild
scream, had left, and there was a chance for the rest of
us to be chalk-marked, all hotel omnibuses had gone for

the night. Nothing remained but a baggage *camion*, on the front seat of which, together with the chauffeur, the Swiss Napoleon, the nurse, and the four children, Titania and I rode triumphantly round the corner to the Casino. Shortly afterward, piloted by a chambermaid, we again found ourselves in open air, under stars, crossing a gravelly courtyard. Quite a surprisingly long journey it seemed. Up a winding stair, in a distant annex, we found some very clean little rooms with a jovial aroma of chlorides and windows opening above the beach. With magical rapidity a tray of hot chocolate and bread and butter was "made mount" from the kitchen, and it fell to me to administer these delights to two small damsels (aged five-and-a-half and three-and-a-half) who had been hastily thrust into one large bed. They gargled down some of the chocolate, inquired eagerly, "Is this France?" and fell into nescience. So I finished the chocolate and the crackly bread with plenty of curly whorls of pale unsalted butter. At about the same time, in the dining room downstairs, one of our fellow passengers was saying, "Some of that doughy French bread? No, thank you!"

I am always for arrivals late at night. You can't see your surroundings, and the next day you wake into a new world. From my bedroom window eight hours later I looked out upon the sunny courtyard of the hotel and an ancient in a blue apron cutting grass with a scythe.

The Casino—where we stayed two weeks—is perhaps a little symbol of the whole matter. There is one wing of the establishment which is the hotel proper, devoted mostly to the one-night ravishment of Americans. But then you pass through a little door into the casino itself and are in France. A terrace with blue tables fronts the harbour and the pebble beach; behind this is a dance hall where a very gay and violent little orchestra gives an *apéritif-concert* every afternoon. The tiny Citroëns and other queer boat-shaped miniature automobiles keep driving through the courtyard, and the *bons bourgeois* of Cherbourg drop in afternoons and evenings for dancing and *petits chevaux* and even (twice a week) a Paramount film shown on a very minute screen. The operator was very proud of his Paramount films, and assured me that America had produced some very great film artists, such as "Bébé Danyelss" and "Guillaume Ar." It took me an appreciable ponder before recognizing the name of the latter. At the *apéritif-concerts*, where you sit with your Raphael-citron or your café-cognac watching the dancing, you enjoy the cheerful French habit of taking the whole family along for an afternoon sip—grandmother, babies, and the dog. It would be nice to believe that the young men are all poets, for those broad-brimmed black hats and something odd about the shape of their trousers certainly suggest it. But all this gay and harmless life of the casino goes on quite apart from the hotel which the tourists see. It is always like that: there is a little door which divides the France that is exposed for the traveller from the France that goes placably about its own concerns.

But of course the real life of the town is across the revolving bridge, past the upper basin where the

Polish square-rigged corvette *Lwow* is lying, past the
docks where the English tramp steamers are taking
daily the endless stream of crates of new potatoes.
Across the bridge you find the taxicabs drawn up, a
compact little squadron, and among them, if you are
fortunate, perhaps you'll find Lucien Le Cornu, kindest
of guides to the enchanting old towns near Cherbourg.
His only sorrow in life is that a hundred and fifty Americans have gone touring in his car and taken photos of
him but have never sent him a print. This has now
been rectified. If you don't find Le Cornu at his
station at the bridge-end, the thing to do is to go to the
Café Continental near by where they'll give him a
coup de téléphone. M. Le Cornu was a godsend to us;
he is friendly, reasonable, a keen enthusiast for the
old architectures of Normandy, and his French has a
special clarity and penetration into the unaccustomed
transatlantic ear. He has a delightful humour too.
Our first week or so at the Casino, we, with four
urchins, were somewhat the oddity of the establishment;
but then arrived a very wealthy New Yorker with six
children, several maids, five cases of Walker-Gordon
milk, and occupied most of the ground floor of the hotel.
The next morning, before he departed for the château
he had rented at Dinard, I saw him musing pensively
among his mountains of impediment which filled the
lobby. This is where M. Le Cornu enters the anecdote,
for a fleet of seven limousines was deployed in the courtyard to transport the party. Four of these were loaded
with the baggage, and of this freight squadron Le Cornu
was commodore. While the passenger detachment

sped to Granville for lunch, Le Cornu halted his heavy quartet at Lessay for a brief *déjeuner*. The four thirsty chauffeurs sat down at the scrubbed wooden tables of the little Hôtel Félix; the natives crowded round to inquire the meaning of these four vehicles packed inside and out with trunks, baby carriages, golf bags, and what not. It must have looked ominously like another flight of King Louis Philippe; and indeed on that very day President Millerand was vacating the Elysée. What is it, what is it? cried the troubled Normans; for the French are always subconsciously prepared for some sort of *crise* or *coup*. Lucien took a long pull at his cider. "Well," he replied gravely, "you've heard of the American kings—the cattle kings, copper kings, petrol kings? This is *le roi des bagages*."

Excellent Lucien! I still seem to hear the clear yelp of his rubber-bulb horn as he twirls through those Norman villages, taking us to Barfleur, or Valognes loved by Barbey d'Aurevilly, to Greville where Millet was born, or past de Tocqueville's château near Cherbourg, which surely ought to be a place of pilgrimage for Americans; or to Bricquebec, whose Trappist cheese you'll do well to sample, and to the Nez de Jobourg, that fine rocky beak blown by the Atlantic wind. Well named Le Cornu: you know the canorous double note of those French motor horns, the exhale and the in.

But we were crossing the bridge and entering the town itself. Perhaps it would tempt the ladies to linger awhile in Cherbourg if I confided, on Titania's authority, that they'll find in the Rue du Bassin one of the world's best coiffeurs; and not to make it too easy

Baedeker Fibbed

I'll only give the translation of his name, Mr. Burning-fire. More frequented by me was the little photograph shop across the way, where I see good Mme. Vaslot's face of almost agonized intensity as she listens wildly to my French, wondering what unforgivable syntax is coming next. Then, with a sudden radiation of light she grasps my intention. I had seen, in her window, a printed placard remarking how many *situations presque inénarrables* can be preserved with a camera. "*Mais, madame,*" I tell her, "*toute la vie, c'est une situation presque inénarrable.*" She applauds. This leads us on to discuss a small dog that is in the shop, who has had his tail cut off flush with his rump. He is trying, in spite of this—can we say handicap?—to express his pleasure in the good society where he finds himself. I attempt to carry on my argument. "*Voici, madame, encore une autre situation presque inénarrable. C'est bien cruel de couper comme ça, le petit chien se trouve embarrassé parce que la queue c'est l'organe des émotions chez les chiens, son organe de sensibilité.*" With a rush of syllables she and M. Vaslot approve this doctrine, and hasten to explain that it is not their animal but a neighbour's. Their pretty young daughter, embroidering behind the *caisse*, is politely trying to smother her grins.

After a round of the bookstores—where perhaps you may be disconcerted to find "Tarzan des Singes" in the window, flanked by "Rip, l'Homme Qui Dormit Vingt Ans"; and where you buy your Petit Larousse, that heavy but indispensable little travelling university—it may well be that you stop in at the American Express

office to say hullo to the agent, Mr. White, and change
some money. If you happen to be interested in books
and plays, Mr. White is just the man to gossip with,
for he used to be chauffeur to Mrs. Deland and also to
Winthrop Ames. Mr. Ames used to have him read
play MSS. now and then, and I was tempted to get his
opinion on a script of my own that was in my trunk;
but he was giving me nineteen and a half francs to the
dollar, and I didn't want to do anything to lower the
rate. Or perhaps Titania lures you into the Grands
Magasins L. Ratti (M. Ratti is the Wanamaker of
Cherbourg) to buy a waist for the Urchin. Here the
hilarity is extreme when it is discovered that French
urchins wear a kind of webbed corset with which their
smallclothes are kept aloft; there was great grievance in
the Urchin's bosom when he was made acquainted with
this garment. I have promised it shall be quietly
dropped overboard before we lift Sandy Hook again.
A little quiet study of the wine merchants' windows provides good suggestions of new vintages to ask for.
Vin d'Anjou, for instance, which costs two francs
twenty-five per bottle in the town, though it rises to
five or seven at the hotel. (At hotels where they cater
to Americans it is hard to get them to serve you *vin
ordinaire*. The little man with the green apron comes
for your order, and unless you are very stiff with him
he'll send you something with a label on it.)

To be perfectly fair all round, Titania and I went one
evening to a meeting, presided over by the Mayor, held
by the *Ligue Nationale contre l'Alcoolisme*, followed by
an uproariously bad movie, "The Double Life of Doc-

tor Moraud." But the film kept breaking and finally they quit with it unfinished, just at the point where the luckless Doctor Moraud, eminent surgeon and secret helot of *eau de vie*, is about to trepan the fractured skull of his son's fiancée; but on the way to the hospital, while his motor was having a *pneu* changed, he has dodged into a groggery to indulge himself. He totters to the operating table with palsied hand . . . here the celluloid snapped again, and the Mayor got up and said that the operator had had such trouble with the machine that they would have to call it off. Without any of the ironical booing we should have expected, the large audience rose calmly and sifted out. The French take their movies very tranquilly and, odd as it may seem, on a warm clear summer evening they prefer sitting outdoors and watching the sunset, fishing along the docks, or sipping the Raphael-citron that is the favourite bourgeois *apéritif*.

In fact, the "light sane joy of life," as Kipling said in his famous poem, is very evident. It seems based on a certain calm acceptance of necessary facts of living, a simple and hardy jocularity in plain pleasures that is sedative to those who have too long accustomed themselves to the Broadway temperament. The stone hamlets of the Cotentin, original home of so many of our race, are now as grey and lichened as Jobourg's Nose itself. There is something very pitiful about those rude thatched dwellings taking shelter under the pent of a gorse-gemmed hill. Life is reduced almost to its animal rudiments; the ruddy old women jogging back from Cherbourg market in their high-wheeled carts have an almost speechless tranquillity, lulled into a warm doze of the wits by the lyric humming of thin little telephone wires in the breeze. The dusty byways are patterned with the nailprints of their frugally bossed footgear; on the very soil one reads the mark of their pious and necessary thrift. Larks, little mounting flutters of song, keep earnestly pushing up the sky for fear it will tumble. By the village churches are the washing pools, always with a cross or sacred effigy to bless the wholesome work; the women kneel to paddle the linen just as they would kneel to pray, and hardly know one from the other; nor does it greatly matter. Surely the great clerics need not be alarmed at the government's withdrawing its embassy from the Vatican: the church's share in French life is not pillared upon embassies. And if they all wear black when they approach the church, what race has more reason to? See the little war monument at Barfleur, where the names of seven Renoufs of one family are written on the stone. It makes one wamble a bit to think of the million villages of Europe, all those frugal people going about their hard and harmless concerns, cutting their hay and arranging their local fêtes with the children riding on a *petit manège* (or merry-go-round) turned by hand, and meanwhile the pride and stupidity and harassment of politicians can slide the whole thing toward fiendish catastrophe. Then one can understand better the grimness of the Communist placards, pasted on the stone walls of country barns, calling on the *ouvrier* and *paysan* to throw out their bourgeois deputies, and hallooing generals in the Chamber as "*assassins*."

Baedeker Fibbed

We spent one long sunny and windy afternoon at the Pentecost horse races, to which all Cherbourg turns out, from the neighbourhood aristocrats with silk hats and field glasses to the old grey-eyed peasant women in their lace-and-linen coifs, and hundreds of the coloured Senegalese troops in their scarlet bellhop caps. These amiable savages are so absurdly like the American elevator boy that it seems grotesque to hear them jabbering French. I suppose they make in a year about what a New York hat-checker pockets on a Saturday night;—but I don't know that they're less happy. One consoling feature of human life is that wherever you go you find the people quite innocently certain that to be where they are and to do what they are doing is the normal and sensible thing.

But as agreeably revealing evidence of the French enjoyment of simple pleasures I clipped a little piece from the Cherbourg paper, describing how *La Musique* of Hainneville, a sort of singing society in the suburbs, made its first picnic of the season. I please myself by translating with faithful literalness:

At 1 hour 30 the musicians, assembled on the Place de la Mairie, announced by the execution of a morsel the approaching departure for Urville; then, in the name of all the members of *La Musique*, a magnificent object of art was offered to the leader, M. Henri Avoine, on the occasion of this first expedition. Very much touched by this gesture of sympathy, M. Avoine renewed his promise to do all his possible to develop and lead to worthiness the work undertaken.

At the issue of this little manifestation, *La Musique* put itself on the road, followed by about 120 persons, whose number continued to augment all the length of the traject, attaining approximately 450 near Querqueville, and that in spite of the storm, menacing more and more.

All went well as far as Urville, where the excursionists arrived toward 4 hours.

Unfortunately the storm, which burst out almost at once, hindered all the world from taking its diversions, whether on the beach or in the various quarters of the coquettish little town of Urville, and one had to content himself, after the crust-breaking, by making a ball in the interior of the spacious restaurant Renard, when it might otherwise have taken place in the open air, in the superb shrubbery of this establishment.

The return effectuated itself in some excellent conditions and without the least incident, the rain having completely ceased to fall and the gaiety not having ceased to prevail during the whole traject. Toward 8 hours 30 *La Musique* reëntered triumphantly into Hainneville, having been acclaimed everywhere on its course, going and coming.

Wherever you wander, through the astoundingly ancient crooked lanes of the town, sometimes among smells that explain the French passion for perfumery, you find yourself led back toward the harbour. To me, since childhood, docks and railway sidings have always been the most fascinating places to prowl; at Cherbourg you have them both in one. Along the *digue* beyond the *gare maritime* one can study the constant movement of the harbour: pilot boats coming in and out, the fishing fleet with amber sails, and also see the restaurant cars cleaning and getting ready to cater to more Americans. Apparently the stewardesses of

those cars live in them and cook their own meals, for
you'll see them, bare-legged, early in the morning,
washing down the woodwork, a little waver of smoke
coming from the kitchen stovepipe.   If it's one of those
bright mornings of early June, as blue as an alcohol
flame, the railway men who are off duty will be down on
the shingle, paddling.   Frenchmen always seem to be
able to take a few hours off during the day to go wad-
ing.   Very likely they are picking up kindling; for
when the Urchin and I wanted a billet of wood to make
a toy boat, we scoured the beach and environs for many
furlongs without finding a single scrap.   Finally we
had to go to the boatyard and beg a small piece left
over from the fishing smack *Bienheureuse Thérèse*
which they were building.   But if you don't find any
bits of wood lying idle on a French beach, neither do you
find any housekeeping refuse.   Some of our American
seaside towns might well be named Cannes.

Cherbourg is justly proud of her harbour and proud
of her shipyards.   When the *Mauretania* was overhauled there lately, on account of a strike in the English
yards, there was great exultation in the town.   Then,
on her first succeeding voyage, a propeller dropped off.
This elicited an editorial in the Cherbourg *Eclair*,
pointing out that no work had been done on the
propellers while the *Mauretania* was in the *chantiers*
of Cherbourg.   In fact, said the editor, perhaps it was
exactly the fact that our Cherbourg workmen *hadn't*
overhauled the *hélices* that caused one of them to
falter under the excessive strain of the hitherto-unheard-
of celerity at which the vast vessel was marching after

the invigorating repairs made to the machine by our expert mechanicians. Local pride, happily, is the same all the world round.

Titania would never quite agree with me as to the fun of patrolling the railway sidings, reading the *étiquettes* on the freight cars. But that is how I learn my French, such as it is. The study of posters, advertisements, municipal notices, all sorts of random *affiches*, I find more useful than a phrase book. I didn't begin to get the hang of the subjunctive until I found it on the label of my matchbox. "*Ne jetez jamais vos allumettes avant qu'elles soient entièrement éteintes.*" And sometimes the bills-of-lading pasted on the sides of freight cars will tell you more truth about what's going on than the daily paper. While some of the journals were expressing alarm that the first thing M. Herriot and his "bolshevik" government would do would be to evacuate the Ruhr, I found freight cars loaded with gun carriages marked for *l'Armée sur Rhin*. For the most part, though, I found those quaint little wagons (with their famous legend *Hommes* 40, *Chevaux* 8) loaded with matters more to my pacific taste: potatoes and carrots from the Farmers' Syndicate of Barfleur, or officers' horses from Saint Lô coming to take part in the races.

Meditation along these docksides gave me excellent opportunity to fortify my verbal resources. Amply provided with nouns of all sorts, my methods of putting them together in trains of speech are as primitive as the French way of shunting freight cars with an elderly horse. It was on the sidings of Cherbourg that I in-

vented my trick to avoid the embarrassment of genders
—always use all nouns in the plural and without qualify-
ing adjectives. Do not say, for instance, *I love this old
church*, for then you've got to know whether "church"
is male or female. Say rather *One loves churches*.
This lends a plain and even a quite lofty flavour to
one's style, full of an 18th-century tincture, a Ben
Franklin aphoristic and moralizing touch that must be
soothing to the French ear. And indeed one is perpetu-
ally charmed by the infinite courtesy with which they
hear us mangle their pronunciations. I was trying to
imagine what would be the English phonetic equivalent
for some of my utterances. When I ask the way to a
village church it probably sounds to the native as
though someone said to me, at home, "Ow wass it
pleeze pozeable for locating ze sharsh?" These
difficulties, and one's necessary limitations to the
simplest formulæ (avoiding all *situations presque
inénarrables*) have their charms, however; particularly
for one whose trade is to deal in language. One uses
one's own tongue so glibly, the words arriving in the
mouth almost unconsciously, that it is an enormous
advantage to study seriously, at a mature age, the
actual hooks and couplings by which a foreign speech
is put together—how, to pursue my railway metaphor,
these little baggage trucks of nouns and adjectives are
made into trains, conjunctioned to the engine of a
verb, and puffed off to carry their cargo to some destination. You find yourself looking (with a new respect)
at an English sentence to remind yourself just how it is
done. Was not one of the secrets of Mr. Conrad's rich

appeal that he always dealt with English in the tenderness of one to whom it came not by birthright but as a long arduous acquisition? So you go about your rounds in the town, picking up a phrase here and there, sticking in a subjunctive now and then for good measure, acquiring the dainty technic of shopping, and blundering in and out of places that look for all the world like square-meal restaurants but which serve only liquids. "Don't the French ever *eat* anything?" cried Titania in despair, one evening when we had tried three or four cafés looking for some supper, but could find nothing but *apéritifs* and music. Of course, one learns the stunts in time; just as the pipe smoker can even learn to inure himself to that Scaferlati tobacco; but at first the instinct of the foreigner leads him with unerring certainty to do the wrong thing.

Our dallying in Cherbourg was not mere indolence, nor due entirely to the picturesqueness of the town. There we were solidly based on two of the very few bathtubs in the Cotentin—a great advantage to travellers with small children—and these large china receptacles constituted our G. H. Q. while prospecting for a summer home farther down the coast. That was why we covered so much country with M. Le Cornu, and as an introduction to French ways of living and thinking I urge house-hunting. You see innumerable domestic interiors of all sorts, and you learn, away from the life of hotels, how wrong are those travellers who insist on thinking of the French as rapacious. I recall one of our early expeditions when we passed a travelling coffee vendor, sitting on his little cart which was being pulled through the dust and hot sunshine by two hardy mongrels. His dogs were both so like an animal I was once greatly attached to, a certain Mr. Gissing, that I couldn't resist asking him if it would *dérange* him if I took a photo. He was quite pleased, cried his dogs to a smart trot, and came gaily along while I snapped the lens. In the subsequent palaver he spoke very fast and with a difficult accent, saying several times that it was very warm, and something about a *bistro* a little farther along the road. This I didn't quite grasp, but supposed he was suggesting that having taken his picture I might now stand him a drink. But when I began to haul out some money I was embarrassed to find that he had been offering to treat *me;* and this though we had spun past him in a car and probably looked to him like millionaires. The situation was painful, but we got by it all right, and he accepted, after some protest, a five-franc note. He said it was too much money for a drink, but I insisted that the dogs also should have one. And at this moment the Urchiness created a diversion by falling into a deep ditch of water hidden in the long grass at the roadside. When we left him our friend was sitting happily at the *bistro,* enjoying—if the sign was to be trusted—*Consommations du Premier Choix.*

By now, of course, settled householders in a Norman village, Titania and I know the essentials of rustic technic. We know how to bicycle into a strange hamlet, pick out the most promising café, and take our lunch sitting at a bare table in the kitchen, looking into the mouth of an enormous fireplace where a kettle of sausages is simmering over a charcoal fire; where the bare table is spread with knives and a huge haunch of bread, and you get your share of the great platter of vegetables that goes round to the teamsters and others who are on the adjoining bench. And you see the copper utensils on the wall, the war helmet in the place of honour over the hearth, and the mother-of-pearl clock. The two-franc *pourboire* you leave behind must not be given as a tip but as a gift to the small girl who watches shyly from the corner. These delicacies of deportment were beyond us in our early days in Cherbourg; but it was M. Le Cornu, I think, who set us on the right road. If you will note what are the hostelries approved by Baedeker, then you can find us at the opposite end of the town. Never, unless you introduce the topic, will your hostess admit that she knows you are foreigners. But she gives away her awareness by one invariable sign: she'll ask you if you would like to have tea with your meal.

And now, as I look back at my memories of Cherbourg, it is evening, that soft, gradual dusk; and though it may be drizzling a bit you stroll along the docks. Across the bridge, now out of use while the lock gates are open, the special train for Paris, crammed with the *Berengaria's* passengers, is just pulling out. Waiting for the bridge to reopen is a whole cross-section of the French provinces: the tiny trolley car with two girls as conductor and driver; the workman with his string bag carrying home two bottles of wine; the market cart with the dog underneath doing his best to help pull; small boys in black pinafores; a woman in *sabots* with a fishing pole; a little Citroën (like a yacht's dinghy on wheels) with a little man in it, equally minute and dapper, on his way to dance and game at the Casino. Those delightful little Citroëns! Even the name sounds fragrant, and I feel sure they ought to smell not of gasoline but of perfumery. Nothing is so precious as those first impressions of a foreign soil; never again are your eyes quite so sharply alert to the valuable comedies of contrast. And those passengers whom I see now, rolling in their lighted compartments toward Paris, may perhaps be right in hastening so wildly toward the capital. But I have a strange feeling that all the breath and essence of France may not necessarily be in Paris; and sometimes one wants to do one's devotions singly, not among other thousands.

And so when the time came to leave Cherbourg it was with the surprised feeling, not at all anticipated, that one had made a new friend, a friend who could not henceforth be omitted from one's happy memories. On that last evening, smoking a pipe along the quay, I met a young man from the real-estate agency who had joined some of our excursions and had been specially patient with our absurdities. We had a stroll together, and his English being about on a level with my French, we promised to correspond each in the other's language. His letter happens to be in reach of my hand, for I have been using it to prop up one leg of my typewriter, the table in the thatched cottage where I am now writing being a bit uneven. I take the liberty of copying a bit of it, as I can think of no better testimony in honour of French friendliness.

Do you remember [he writes], of the nice evening passed in Jobourg? A evening like that one was too short. Yes, because it is always very tedious to leave some nice people. I think the little Christopher [he means the Urchin] is pleased to pass her holidays in the beautiful country of the France. I want he must be enjoying of the France and of the French people for he must be latter a friend of the France. I think, dear sir, that you can manage with your French. I think so because you speak already very well. May be after your stay in France it shall be impossible for you to speak English. It must not.

I am pleased to send you this little letter and be sure if you may be I am a friend for you.

I think that the typewriter will march very steadily with that little wad of affectionate simplicity for a support. A common phrase in France nowadays is *"Plutarch a menti"*—"Plutarch lied." You see the book of that title in all the bookshops. And, as far as Cherbourg is concerned, Baedeker lied too.

WHEELS ON PARNASSUS

THE bicycle, the bicycle surely, should always be
the vehicle of novelists and poets. How pleasant
if one could prove that a decline in literary delicacy
followed the disappearance of the bike from American
roads. After eleven years without one, here I am in a
country where the bicycle abounds. My memory returns to old Shotover, the tall green curio I bought
in England in 1910. She had a queer double frame,
much stared at by rustics from Basel to Auld Reekie,
from the Cotswolds to the Wash. Delightful British
pushbikes, some of them even used to have multiple
gears. Not that I am disloyal to the automobile.
For I know the peculiar thrill of motor cars, how one
learns to love the steady drumming of their faithful
organs, the gallant arch of the hood as it goes questing,

like a sentient creature, along dazzling roads. Yet in a car you are carried; on a bike you go. You are yourself integral with the machine.

The bicycle is to me a kind of symbol of those old careless days long ago. How cheering to find still posted, on country inns in France, the emblem of the Cyclists' Touring Club, of which one was once a member, and whose little identification card was accepted (Oh, simple days!) as a passport. One always sought out the hostelries with that sign, because they were supposed to give the members a reduced rate for "bed and breakfast." And how they hated to do it. One wonders if the young French person on that Rhine steamer remembers herself of the three eccentric youths with the C. T. C. badges. She was a damsel of rather free manners, just the kind of person Jean Jacques was always encountering on his travels. The C. T. C. emblems roused her curiosity, and she asked what they were. "Mademoiselle," replied one of the trio, "it is the Club Terrestre de la Chasteté."

And speaking of the C. T. C., has everyone forgotten the jolly old L. A. W.—the League of American Wheelmen? That too had its literary flavours, for was not Mr. S. S. McClure editor of its magazine?

It is when you come back to bicycling, after long dispractice, that you realize how exquisite a physical art it is. Once more that strong tightness of the thigh muscles, once more the hot sun on the shoulder blades, the odd shift in bodily *tenue* when you have to push on foot up a long hill (comparable to the flatness of walking after skating, or that uneasiness in a ship in still

harbour after days at sea). As you spin down aisles
of hedgeway you can ponder the daintily equilibrated
poise that makes those two wheels your obedient Sia-
mese twins. I read once of a savage chief in Africa
who was given an old bicycle and a top hat, in exchange
for a caravan of ivory, I suppose. He traversed the
sunbaked paths near his village riding the one and
wearing the other, hallooing with innocent glee. I can
understand his feelings. If one wears a hat at all
while biking it might as well be the silk cylinder of
fashion, to express a sense of psychic and carnal welfare.
In a recent play, "Roger Bloomer," one of the characters remarked, "I wear a silk hat as a charm against
passion." The bicycle also is an amulet against various
disorders. To see before one a forked or meandering
road, a wedge-towered Norman church in the valley,
to explore the fragrance of lanes like green tunnels,
to hear the whispering hum beneath you and the rasp
of scythes in a hayfield, all this might well be homœo-
pathic against passion, for it is a passion itself.

But these letters are adjured to have some bearing
on literary matters. So let's take this turning on the
left (which leads across links toward the sea) and sit
on the dunes to think out our rearward idea. A warm
southwest gale is creaming the surf on to the beach;
the sandy turf, sheep-cropped, is speckled with small
pink and yellow flowers.

An odd feeling comes sometimes to a writer who has
long carried in the knapsack of the mind some notion
that he wants to put in ink. It is a sensation I can only
describe as Getting Ready to Write. Those phantoms

[37]

of imagination, so long halted frozen in mid-gesture,
begin to show marks of animation. In my particular
case, it is now four and a half years that I have seen
them sitting in their absurd unchanged attitudes. No
wonder they are stiff: one of them (what a dear she is!)
told me her foot had gone to sleep. They are sitting
round a table, it is a birthday party. You would think
that the cake must be very stale by this time, the little
red candles guttered out. But no: I can see them burning steadily, the bright untrembling candles of a dream.
Even in the puppet postures where I left them I can
see those phantoms strangely show an air of expecta-
tion. Something must be done about it.

In these moods bicycling seems perfectly the right
employ. It is all very well to say to yourself that
you are not thinking as you wheel serenely along; but
you *are*, and that sure uncertainty of the cyclist's
balance, that unconsciously watchful suspension (solid
on earth yet so breezily flitting) seems to symbolize
the task itself. The wheel slidders in a rut or on a
slope of gravel: at once, by instinct, you redress your
perpendicular. So, in the continual joy and disgust
of the writer's work, he dare not abandon that difficult
trained alertness. How much of the plain horror and
stupidity is he to admit into his picture? how many of
the grossly significant minutiæ can he pause to include?
how often shall he make a resolute fling to convey that
incomparable energy of life that should be the artist's
goal above all? These are the airy tinkerings of his
doubt: and as he passes from windy hill-top to green
creeks and grazings sometimes the bicycle sets him

free. He sees it all afresh: nothing, nothing has ever been written yet: the entire white paper of the world is clean for his special portrait of all hunger, all joy, and all vexation. In the sunny market-place, sitting on a warm stone under the statue of the *poilu*, he feels that noble thrill of living and being surrounded by similar life. Even ants in an ant-hill feel it too, I dare say.

Blundering with a foreign language there sometimes comes a moment when you find, astonished, that you have talked for a few sentences fluently and without conscious choice. Just so, in unexpected purities of feeling, you are aware that for an instant you might almost have stammered a phrase or two of the strangest foreign tongue, the universal cryptograms of beauty that legislatures are too busy to hear. This was the language, for instance, that Llewelyn Powys glimpsed between the lines when he read Matthew Arnold in the wilderness of Africa. He tells about it in his glorious "Black Laughter," a book richly written, with the savour of an old, old speech; one of those rarest of books, a book written not in dialect but in English sound and sparkling from the ancient cellars of the language.

So you climb on your bicycle again, renewing in your nostrils the summer sweetness of this divine and anxious land, and swim off with the Southwest at your back. What a book it would be if one could truly write just a straight record of one human farce. What an audacious book, with the title "For I So Loved the World."

THE BENEDICTINE STYLE

SURROUNDED in and by a foreign language, we become the more sharply conscious of our own. Studying books, newspapers, even random scraps of advertisement and *affiche*, intent to discern exactly how this ingenious palaver conveys itself, a gruesome thought arrives. Suppose there were, somewhere, an earnest foreigner, ill acquaint with English, carefully reading *us*, and wondering plaintively (perhaps with his dictionary handy) whether our stuff is pure and good; as a means of communication, that is. We are suddenly aware that in our own tongue most of us hardly know whether we are writing "well" or not. And we resume, all the more determined to root out the essential qualities of French style, our study of the nearest text, which happens to be the circular wrapped round the neck of this bottle of Benedictine we are opening. It reads agreeably enough.

La partie active de la véritable Bénédictine est presque exclusivement composée de plantes croissant sur les falaises de Normandie, récoltées et infusées au moment de la sève et de la floraison.

That seems straightforward and plain. Some of the prettiest of the *falaises de Normandie* are right in front of this house; we take our sunset stroll there every evening.

Ces herbacées par leur voisinage de la mer, encore toutes saturées de brome, d'iode et de chlorure de sodium, développent et conservent dans les liquides spiritueux et sucrés, leurs principes vivifiants et salutaires.

We understand now why the skylarks sing so wittily over those rocky cliffs. But we begin to be a little leery of the *Anciens Moines Bénédictins de l'Abbaye de Fécamp* as stylists. They are what Frank Adams has called Coupling Kates. They are never satisfied with a celibate noun, verb or adjective.

On peut ainsi résumer ses qualités: Netteté de goût, onctuosité franche et bien fondue. . . . Nul aussi n'a jamais contesté ses vertus antiapoplectiques, apéritives, digestives et antispasmodiques; lorsqu'elle est étendue d'eau.

There is much here to ponder, we conclude, as we take our coffee in the garden. How, in literary matters, is one to attain distinction of taste, combined with a frank and well-founded unctuosity?

The Romany Stain

We come next upon M. Abel Bonnard, the occasional essayist of the *Journal des Débats*, who gently chides the President of the Republic for the formula he used in opening the Olympic games. M. Doumergue said, "*Je proclame l'ouverture des Jeux olympiques.*" M. Bonnard suggests that "*Je déclare ouverte*" would have been "more sober and more lapidary." It is evident that M. Bonnard must be heeded; he has lately been awarded the *Grand Prix de Littérature* by the French Academy. He is disturbed by the slovenly use of language in some official quarters, particularly the wireless operator on the Eiffel Tower, whose verbal taste is not as lofty as his station in life. A Tower of Babel, evidently. But happy man and happy nation, still to expect some classic gusto of speech even in politics. We Americans certainly count on our spokesmen being sober; but not lapidary—not in any literary sense.

So it is delightful to see how prompt the French are to reproach—among themselves—the negligent use of their language. I pick up Professor Strowsky's "Renaissance Littéraire de la France Contemporaine," and find him tackling even so well-known a writer as M. Pierre Benoit:

Le français de M. Benoit n'est pas toujours très sûr. Qui peut se vanter d'écrire un français impeccable? Personne? Si, cependant! Celui qui, ayant pour ami un écrivain difficile et attentif, se confie entièrement à cet ami. Celui-ci a des chances de parler français. Puisque M. Pierre Benoit admire Jules Tellier, qu'il me permette de lui dire combien Tellier était attentif et sévère, pour soi et pour les autres! Je sais un écrivain, aujourd'hui justement illustre, dont il épluchait phrase à phrase, et mot à mot, le style, pour le rendre impeccable. Et cet écrivain acceptait avec une vive reconnaissance ces corrections minutieuses et implacables. M. Benoit a besoin d'un tel ami.

This charmingly expresses the seriousness with which the French consider literary deportment. To them, perhaps, the very highest virtue resides in a quality that, *chez nous*, has become sometimes a term of disregard, "academic." I shall not expose my own thoughts about Professor Strowsky's suggestion. But it is interesting to consider, suppose one did want to submit a MS. to some American writer, to be impeccabled, "picked over, phrase by phrase," whom would you trust? I should like to see Doctor Canby give us a list.

Our ignorances of one another's languages lead to many situations that are hilarious; but also, among those whose business it is to manœuvre important affairs, to awkward moments. When the British premier was in Paris the other day to confer with M. Herriot, a quaint thing happened—at least, if the reporter of the *Echo de Paris* is to be trusted. Mr. MacDonald, worn out after exhausting conferences, was ready to leave the Quai d'Orsay to catch his train for Calais. The motor car was waiting. He climbed in. The French premier, eager to show his guest every courtesy, intended to drive with him to the station. But in the flurry of the moment M. Herriot had come out bareheaded. "Wait a minute, I'll get my

hat and stick," he said—in French, of course. "I'm
going with you." But the interpreter, whose duties
were over, wasn't there. Mr. MacDonald did not
understand. M. Herriot rushed for his hat, but when
he returned a moment later the car was already driving
off. He had to find a taxi and hasten after it. Now
this tiny incident may have been tinted by the reporter
of a paper which is not very generous toward either
of these statesmen. But it's the kind of thing that
might happen and does happen in human affairs, and
on which, sometimes, great destinies depend. In the
less momentous circles where the interests of *littérateurs*
revolve, our mutual ignorances are equally deplorable.
I read, in a speech made by M. André Chevrillon—who
understands English literature so intimately—that de
Musset's "Lorenzaccio" is "*la tragédie la plus shakes-
péarienne qui ait été écrite depuis Shakespeare en aucune
langue.*" If that is true, why had we not been told
so more often; or at any rate more effectively? I suppose it is because even in the parliaments of literature
there are always occurring so many "exclamations, di-
verse movements, and noise at the extreme Left," as
the French papers describe sessions of the Chamber of
Deputies.

It is odd how one evening's desultory reading will
often seem to keep itself in the same channel. Before
my eyelids dropped their shade—do I have to put in
the quotation marks?—I happened upon a brief account
of a speech made by a well-known Frenchman at a
banquet of an organization that abbreviates itself
"The U. C. B. B. A." I shall not attempt to unlace

The Benedictine Style

the initials. But the paragraph deserves *verbatim* traduction for students of the human comedy.

M. ——, greeted by the acclamations of the extremely numerous attendance, congratulated the U. C. B. B. A. for its vitality and progress, emphasizing with powerful eloquence that in the dangerous crisis which confronts contemporary society, the essential task is to restore personal, domestic, professional, and social morality, and that it is precisely this task of salvation that the U. C. B. B. A. so happily pursues.

So there is one kind of style that is current in all languages. I fear that to describe it we have to fall back on our old Benedictines of Fécamp. Frank unctuosity . . . *étendue d'eau.*

THE SENSE OF SIGNIFICANCE

THE field at the top of the cliff, overlooking the sea,
has been shaved; cut down to short, soft stubble,
blanched and sweetened by the sun. The skylarks who
nested in those cool tangles of long grass have moved
elsewhere, I suppose; perhaps to the fairy isles of Chausey that notch the western brim. Chausey might
well be a sort of Penguin Island. After watching
its purple stains on the skyline through a month
of clear sunsets, it was rash to pay them actual visit.
Rewarded rashness, though, for even in a drizzle there
was no disillusion in those seaweed-matted clumps
of granite, joined by webs of sand into one continent
at the ebb, insulated again at high tide, a sprinkle of
surf-banged crags. A tiny strait serves as harbour for a
few smacks; there is an abandoned fort (of Napoleon III's

era); a stone chapel with the customary ship model hanging as flattery to the gods of gale. Even the dour château of M. Renault, the automobile magnate, suggests that special tinge of feeling that one describes as Romance. One remembers it was not far away, in similar scenes, that Victor Hugo found his "Travailleurs de la Mer."

So the blue scissorings of Chausey, seen from our seaward cliff at sunset, have not lost by visit their fairyland suggestion. Even are they more precious by memory of the homeward voyage, when the *Mouette* (an open launch of fifty feet, carrying one sail) wallowed and capered in a drenching southwester. Unsheltered, the crowded passengers sat trickling, and in more violent rollings were hardly appeased by the master's remark "*N'y a pas de danger, n'ayez pas peur!*" Always alert for the frolic French subjunctive, I remembered that it is used chiefly in expressions suggesting uncertainty and doubt. Ladies were ill, even quite hardy masculines aware of that quaint impulse to yawn which is the token of an entrail not wholly stable. But excellent is the stoicism of the Gaul. A stout grizzled gentleman wearing the ribbon of Madagascar campaigns many years ago, who had lunched on shrimps, rhubarb confiture, *Calvados* (brandy made from cider), and other notables of Norman picnicking, was faintly tinct with green under his summer tan. Yet when a special spout of spray came inboard down his nape, he merely shifted a little on sopping quarters and remarked "*Ce n'est pas chic.*" He is a rather famous Parisian modiste, which somehow makes his phrase all the more pleasant. The tall cliffs of Granville were a welcome sight looming through pelting squalls, as our *Mouette* came boiling and staggering under their lee.

On these grassy headlands, idly watching the profile of the old fortressed rock a mile away, there is much to ponder which is not idle. Studying the long bend of the gulf beneath, the various tinting of sea, the brown-purple shadow masses in distant scarps of cliff, a writer is tempted to envy the pictorial artist who has his fundamental material so seizable, so suggestive, so takeably to hand. The story-teller's job seems desperately more nebulous. Totally from gossamer nothing, your effect shall be contrived; without even the dexterous physical amusement that helps to keep the painter absorbed and happy. Against that sword-coloured sky, vast with the empty glimmer of evening, you are promptly aware of human mirth and movement as a silhouetted pattern. How, out of all that confusing richness, to choose the exactly necessary trifles that will propose the desired emotion? One can only fall back on the instinctive Sense of Significance, that subtle and massive intuition that must be (for every type of creator, I suppose) the captain of his seven deadly senses.

The Sense of Significance! Yes, that occult and instantaneous decision that certain gestures, certain random incidents, are necessary parts of the artistic composition of our own world. This instinct is capricious and quick, often one is puzzled to know why such petty observations come full of meaning, magically confluent with the dark undercurrent of the mind. I can only illustrate by mentioning shortly a few poor silly glimpses that seemed to me lately (I did not know why) to have peculiar magic. It is hard to be so terse; but as that excellent Abel Bonnard said the other day, "*Il n'est pas mauvais de s'exercer à parler en bref de ce qu'on aime.*"

At Plymouth: my first sight of England in eleven years. The *Lancastria* at anchor under the green steeps where Drake played the world's most famous game of bowls. Coming down the cabin alley I saw a gull poised outside. He floated there on wings, framed in the brass circle of the porthole, looking at me with a cruel fanatical eye. Just behind him was the little harbour where the *Mayflower* set sail. Was there accusation in his look? "What have *you* done to justify the faith of those tough yachtsmen?"

On a great spread of beach at low tide: a warm vacant afternoon, the smell of hay blowing down from the cliffs mixed with the strong acid of the sea. Far above, continual twitter of larks, the ear unconsciously sharpening itself to follow their wiry tinkle to the height where it blurs with your own blood-stroke. In that sunny vacuum of feeling, a chime from the church a mile away. The wave of deep sound booms overhead. Then, after the passage of the note, a smaller following vibration, an actual quaver of air felt rather than heard, a magically secret ripple in the blue, the gently churning wake of those thick pushing clangs. That infinitesimal tremble, swimming in soft space, was like hearing the actual movement of some strange law of life. A French lady told me the other day that on that beach, in a certain slope of sunlight, she had seen one of the bathers apparently surrounded by a halo of brightness. I know that one afternoon I went far along the coast, toward a weatherbeaten house that stands solitary by the sea. It had beckoned me since I first saw its outline in the distance. When I got near it I recognized it at once. I had seen that same house, or at least one sufficiently like it, a year before, in a dream.

A heavy tinker's wagon, drawn by one horse. Underneath, harnessed to the axle, a small terrier, pulling mightily, doing his best to help along. His tongue hung dripping, he strained fiercely at his leather hitchings, his tail curled upward with delighted enthusiasm. Why did that dog suddenly strike me as full of parable? I looked again. The wagon was going down a steep hill, and both horse and tinker were doing their best to hold back the load against the grade. But their valiant consort was still doing his forward possible, as usual.

Bicycling in a green woodland, round a corner I found a little avenue among trees. Bordered with flowers it led to an oddly fantastic house, an old stone mansion that had been built over with modern additions. And above the front door, a large statue of seated Buddha. Reading Montaigne one afternoon in the garden, I heard a melancholy chanting outside the wall, the slow shuffle of feet passing by. So many songs and oddities go down a French village road that pres-

The Sense of Significance

ently one is too incurious to look out; besides, I was absorbed in the good old gentleman's apologies for his stupidity, his ignorance even of the names of the vegetables in his garden. But I heard our old Julie click the latch and look out. What is it? I called. She came to me with a grave face. "A funeral," she said; and added, with a certain relish, "*Un enterrement de première classe.*"

But nor sunset ponderings, nor reading Montaigne, will help one much in trying to set in order the task that he has planned. These things abide the fortune of the inkwell. Even Montaigne must sometimes have laboured and brought forth a mouse.

THE LATIN QUARTER

I

IT'S amusing to come back after twelve years to the little book-lined Rue de la Sorbonne with its tinny chimes and tiny hotels; and to find the old Gerson, that seemed so darkly wicked and Murgeresque in one's student era, really so placid and respectable. How adorably satanic we believed it in those rainy spring days of 1912! Even the staircase was an *escalier à tire-bouchon:* a corkscrew—six steep spirals to be climbed, but a real *gradus ad Bohemiam* which gave an agreeable sense of unbottling the bright vintage of hilarity; though the three young men in the attics had little need of real corkscrews. Cocoa was their frugal brew, cooked for themselves. With excited awe they gazed into that grimy little courtyard at the rear, where a young woman used to come to the window, in occasional lustres of sunshine, to shake out her long hair and bask herself in smallclothes. She had merely been shampooing, I dare say: but these lads asked themselves, with all Mark Twain's eagerness, was this the fabled *grisette?* But there are few Rapunzels nowadays. That virginal notion of the gay sinfulness of Paris, inalienable conviction of every Anglo-Saxon youth, can never quite be recaptivated. The transplanted Greenwich Villagers who are said to frequent the *Dôme* and the *Rotonde* probably degust the same ecstasy. The half-world (so those logical students of 1912 figured it) would naturally be divided into two quarters—the Latin Quarter and Montmartre. They spent their time coasting from one to the other, occasionally pausing (in purple jacket and velvet *béret*) at the American Express office, to give the despised "tourists" a valuable glimpse of Life with the dotted *i*. Their spirit was as engagingly frolic as that of the fellow in blue jerkin and asses'-ears hood who rides the donkey in the Parchment Fair painting in the cloister of the Sorbonne. If it had been customary to express devotion to this university by sweaters with a large S on the chest, I feel sure they would have worn them. They knew nothing of *Dômes* and *Rotondes:* they wrote their letters at the Café de la Source on the Boule' Mich', because Stevenson had done so at their age. Because they were young libertads, they went to hear Jaurès. . . . And now Le Penseur has left the Panthéon and Jaurès is going there. Murger and de Musset and Baudelaire aren't what the young Latin Quarter reads now: it reads André Gide. I was going to say something about M. Gide's "Corydon," but I have just seen a little troop of clear-eyed and divinely placid American librarians trotting reverently into the Panthéon. I prefer not to disturb them with the odd matters that French intellectuals discuss.

It is in a different spirit that the twelve-years-older student revisits the Latin Quarter, the Promised Land of booksellers, where each byway seems one more shelf in an endless library. Certainly not in a disillusion, but in a changed illusion; for life, I hope, is a series of gently shifting hallucinations. The Latin Quarter, where we students feel so instinctively *chez nous*, still has its divine magic. Still, absurdly enough, the sight of those innumerable books, or the pale statue of Comte, the pensive stone faces of Pasteur and Victor Hugo, thrill us to adventure more burningly our own imagined toils. But we carry in our pocket nowadays a little roll of *papier gommé transparent* to mend the brittle ten-franc notes that have such a way of coming in half. It's a kind of symbol.

We have had—in these twelve years—to mend so many scraps of paper with transparent adhesives. We have learned that even the brave life of literature and the arts has its hokums and trickeries. That it is not always the man with the most conical beard and broadest-brimmed black hat who is the greatest poet. Even the Quarter no longer proclaims the Rights of Man, "in the presence of the Supreme Being," quite so confidently as in 1791 or thereabouts. We have learned that—even along the sacred Boule' Mich'—the best-known products of the American arts are Jackie Coogan, J. O. Curwood, Wrigley's *"friandise à mâcher,"* and . . . "Esquimaux Brick!" (Poor old Esquimaux Pie! Who would have expected to find it resurrected here?) And we note that the *Nouvelles Littéraires* can be just as carelessly proof-read and as full of pseudo-critical tripe as any of our own literary organs.

But do these little gummed transparencies invalidate our legal tender? Not a bit! Our dreams and amusements are all the merrier. We revel in the ingenuity of fraudulent book-jackets, admiring their sheer genius —*Ce récit galant narquois, qui nous revèle les intimités féminines, fait songer à certains contes du XVIIIme siecle. Il en a la forme agréable, la psychologie furtive, les audaces élégantes*. We almost pray for a rainstorm, to perfect the luxury of browsing in the book porches of the Odéon. If, in a famous theatre whose green-room is placarded with photos of managers and authors, enchantingly bearded, who *look* so like great artists, we encounter only a dull, dirty farce, does it not set one dreaming all the more valiantly of the piece one imagines from one's own inkpot? If one's eyes were always in the shop windows, one would miss the little coop on the pavement where an ingenious bartender has put a kennel with a trough of running water— Louigi's Dog's Bar, he calls it. The French are on much more intimate terms with dogs than we, and talk to them more understandingly. Compare Senator Vest's unholy palaver with what Charles Baudelaire wrote in "Petits Poèmes en Prose."—That the French have at least one frankly canine trait, I need not insist.

How one would like to condense, into a few hundred words, the exquisite flavour of the Quarter. In those

The Romany Stain

quiet streets round St. Sulpice I study the windows of undertakers, stationers, pastry cooks, ecclesiastical publishers and tailors. How delightful it must be to get a bill from a French doctor. Thus he goes about it:

LE DOCTEUR G. RIBAUT

prie..................................
d'agréer l'expression de ses sentiments
les plus distingués et suivant l'usage,
lui adresse le note de ses honoraires
s'élevant à la somme de.................

Or, if you are a parson and want a new hat, one of those sublime shallow-crown black platters, how pleasant to be able to get one that is marked *Dernier Style*. What business has a priest got worrying about the latest style in cassocks and soup-plate hats? This bothered me. In the vacation silence of the Sorbonne corridors, a familiar kind of protest is scrawled on the wall. We can translate it, gently, by "The examiners who flunked me are swine." The incessant ringing of the tramways keeps one hungry: they sound like boarding-house dinner bells at home. One goes back to the little coffee-bar, where the rolls are always waiting, split and buttered, in a neat crisscross pile, on the zinc counter.

But what is the reason of that curious intellectual exultation that the Quarter gives, that fecundity of impulse it offers to the artist, that sense that the mind is in its birthright element? I think you find its secret best in the Luxembourg gardens. Behind the flamboyant formality of the flower beds, behind the charming heedlessness and enjoyment, is a strange flavour of peaceful melancholy, of incredulity, of impossible hopes. Utterly different from New York, where the mind flows with the moment, here it seems as it were to touch bottom psychologically. There is a background of enchanted despair. The toy yachts are becalmed in the basin and will never come to port. The Medici fountain smells of sodden leaves and is a grand place to be sad. The great dusky Polyphemus looms over the sprawling lovers as the great laws of life eavesdroop over us all—proclaiming in the presence of the Supreme Being! The young men in black hats are goaded by the most unpleasant passions! (I refer you to M. Gide.) Outside the Comédie Française (the Comedy!) our darling de Musset's statue reminds us that the songs of despair are the sweetest of all.

I wonder if I'm wrong? I'm not trying to express my own feelings, which are trivial and don't matter. I am trying to serve as a film to photostat the genius of the place. In these brilliant Luxembourg flower beds I seem specially aware of this ancient channel of feeling in which emotions run. The Quarter is rich ground for the thinker because it has perfected, and made gracious and proud, the art of being unhappy.

II

I am waiting to hear the chime of the Sorbonne church strike eleven: I wanted to hear it again, to get the right word for it. *Tinny*, which I used last year, is certainly not right. It is a light, cool, insouciant little chime; but I don't catch the just adjective, and can only

advise you to listen for it yourself. It is not ponderous
nor monitory nor deeply musical: in fact it seems (as I
suppose is natural in a Latin Quarter belfry) hardly a
religious voice at all. It has in it something of the accent of Ronsard, something of Diderot, and just a faint
clatter of glassware from the zinc café-bar round the corner. I will leave it at that, or it will use up all my space.

Paris would hardly be Paris for me if I didn't hear
the Sorbonne bells; though it is disconcerting to hear
them striking while you are writing an article: another
fifteen minutes gone and you have only descended a
dozen lines. And this ground-floor room at the corner
of the Place (in case there are ladies in the audience)
is the perfect chamber for high-spirited young women.
For, if the toy *ascenseur* is "immobilized for repara-
tions," as sometimes happens, there are no stairs to
climb; and the passage outside our door is one long
stretch of mirrors, where Titania can walk up and
down adjudging the effect of a new hat just arrived
from Mme. Sorbier in the rue Lafayette. But it
grows very chilly toward midnight at the end of
September. *Chauffage Centrale* has a genial sound on
the notepaper; but when, one wonders, does it begin?
If it hadn't been for my well-loved *zinc* (as you are to
call a small bar of that sort, pronouncing it *zank*) which
is warm and bright and full of Chinamen playing cards,
I should hardly have enlivened my fingers enough
to write this letter. But the café-crême with cognac
only costs ten cents, and makes the most intimate of
chauffages centrales.

I understand now why the Quarter spends its evenings

in the cafés—to keep warm. I should have liked to bring in a small electric heater; but the list of prohibitions placarded on the wall is peremptory:—

> All degradations in the rooms are at the charge of the guest. It is forbidden: to do cooking in the rooms, to wash linen, to branch any apparatus on the electric canalization and to modify in whatever it may be the existing installations, to introduce any animal or to make cooking come in from outside.

I haven't really much gift for loitering in cafés. I wish I had: for then I might be able to find out, what has always disquieted me, whether the Boule' Miche' prowlers who look so like poets really are. The fellow with the yellow raincoat, and yellow ringlets as long and curly as Bonny Prince Charley's; and the other fellow with the sleek bobbed hair, the tight-waisted coat, the monocle and cane and open polo-shirt; they are still strolling the pavement just as they were a year ago. What I want to know is, how many poems have they written in the meantime? I always have a horrid fear that they will prove to be merely commissionaires for the Phiteesi shoe-store that appals my eye in that sacred precinct; heaven only knows how profound a disillusion it was to my spirit to find that word Phiteesi in the Latin Quarter: fortunately even the most learned doctors of the Sorbonne probably don't suspect its meaning. But a man who has strength enough left to wrestle against disillusion has not really been damaged; his fancy dives inward and becomes more precious. I cling desperately to the hope that the Chinamen are not the only romantic figures along the Boulevard; that the

young men whose signed photographs are thick over
the comfortable fireplace in Sylvia Beach's charming
bookshop ("To dear Sylvia with just oceans of love")
really are geniuses; that these Murgerian profiles are
truly libertines and literary critics. You remember
O. Henry's little story about the hayseed who looked so
obviously a hayseed that no bunco-man dared go after
him. But he really was a hayseed. And Walt Whitman teaches me to be cautious. Walt would have been
very miserable along the trottoir of the Boule' Miche',
for no one would have noticed him. Yet, though he
looked so like a poet that few good Philadelphians
would touch him, he really was one.—And I don't even
believe that Walt's French, deservedly merrimented by
his readers, was any worse than that of the average
American in Paris.

But I love to think of the young American of the
better sort who comes, like the *naïf* scholar-gipsy he is,
to make his pilgrimage to Paris. It is delightful to
think of him, scandalized in small things that he may
be, if he has understanding, uplifted in great. He has
heard that the book-boxes along the Quais are the shrine
of priest and philosopher; and the statue of Voltaire
grins delightedly at his amazement to find the work
most prominently displayed is "Fleshly Attraction,
Translated from the French," carefully wrapped in
strong twine. For that is the kind of delightful Vanity
Fair and cheapjackery the world is: surely the photo-
graph-pimp wouldn't work so hard unless real Beauty
were near by; nor would it be worth while for so many
people to dress like poets unless the sources of real

poetry were just around the corner. And I doubt if my imagined pilgrim ever buys "Les Belles Flagellantes de New-York" even if he sees it every day on his way toward the Place Vendôme to ask for mail. If he has the jocund humour I like to credit him with, he has a smile when he goes into an antique-shop in the Boulevard St. Germain where he has seen some fine 18th-century leather-bound 12-mos in the window. He finds that they have been gutted to make cigarette-boxes, though still preserving, outwardly, their booklike appearance. He exclaims a little in protest at old books having been served so—"Ah," says the young woman, "they were only religious books."

The sapient pilgrim, if he were wise, would serve an apprenticeship in the provinces; he should be forbidden even to approach Paris until he had learned such elementary rules as never to allow a bottle of wine to be plunged into an ice-bucket—as the Paris restaurants have debauched themselves into doing under the notion that Americans like everything iced. He should avoid the eyes of Rue de la Paix jewellers peering fixedly over their velvet window-curtains, and should gaze in fascinated horror at the engravers' shops where Egyptian princes have their visiting cards displayed and among them the imposing pasteboard

MONSEIGNEUR GLASS
BISHOP OF SALT LAKE

He should learn first, what the cosmopolitan glamour of Paris is not so likely to teach, something of the unspoiled simplicities of the French countryside. It

would do him no harm to hunt out the French equivalent of the old lady from Dubuque. Then he will be
capable, I think, of distinguishing the true Paris, who
makes herself so scarce for untutored eyes. Then he
will see that, faithful to her old motto, this real Paris,
loved by all the world's lovers, fluctuates but is never
merged. He won't waste his clear sunsets at some
rowdy café but will see the little flotilla of toy yachts
skimming the Luxembourg basin. Where the woman
with a bunch of balloons stands at the head of the steps,
the light pours through her red and blue globes; seen
down the gold-bronze avenue they are translucent like
floating jewels. And that mysterious sound of horses'
hoofs that often comes at midnight down the narrow
rue de la Sorbonne, will grow to have its mystic meaning. It is the tramp of some pilgrim cavalcade; it is
the students of the world, coming as they always came,
in faith and hope and gaiety, to the doors of the Sorbonne. Loved as perhaps no other city has ever been
loved, our illusions are worthy of her.

THE WORKS OF M. CHAIX

M. PROUST has been greatly complimented on his rich treatment of the scruples of human psychology, but there is another French writer, widely read, who is also a master of infinitesimal detail. I refer to M. Chaix, the author (or at any rate compiler) of the Livrets-Chaix, a series of volumes not less endless than M. Proust's, and conscientiously revised and re-issued every month or so. M. Chaix's books are not only full of useful information and romantic suggestion, but they are also a whole compendium of French ways of thinking. How charmingly he expresses the French passion for minute codification, for getting things logically arranged and stated. M. Chaix is the real encyclopædist of etiquette—of getting things ticketed.

And he makes you read between the lines; between vertical lines, indeed; for his books are time-tables.

But oh, much more than mere time-tables. M. Chaix's *livrets* (one for each railway company) are a synopsis of his nation's genius for getting things down in black and white—and then going ahead as may be most convenient. The French like to have a thing in writing, just to get it out of the way; not necessarily to adhere to it. Every time you buy a ticket at a French railway station you are reminded (by a placard) that according to the law of 1791 the vendor is not compelled to make change if not convenient. This gives you quite a thrill, seems to take you back to the days of Thermidor and Humidor and Cuspidor. But as a matter of fact, you will always get your change.

M. Chaix has the austerity of a great artist. People like John Ruskin and Henry Adams will try to spoil Mont St. Michel and Chartres for you by putting *their* thoughts into your head. But M. Chaix is never intrusive. All the loveliest places in France are mentioned in his works, but he never tells you what you ought to think about them. He confines himself to the real essentials, viz., how and when you can get there. Henry Adams will din you with his charming palaver about soaring gothic; but M. Chaix soberly states that the trains reach Mont St. Michel at 13:15, 18:5 and 19:30. He evidently worked it out with Mme. Poulard, the innkeeper, as those are just the times to order an omelet. Not a sparrow falls to the ground, by which I mean to say not a traveller misses a connection, but M. Chaix knows why it shouldn't have happened. He probably tried to "effectuate his transit" by way of Versailles Chantiers, where (if he had read the footnote on page 37) only first-class passengers without baggage were admitted to that train.

But I must give you (Oh! for more ample space) some notion of M. Chaix's attention to detail. It is he who makes plain the uplifting influence of American passengers upon dining-car tariffs. Lunch and dinner in the wagon restaurant, *vin non compris*, cost 7 francs and 12 francs; but in the boat trains, 18 francs. On the boat trains, wine costs $7\frac{1}{2}$ francs a bottle as against 3.25 in the regular expresses. M. Chaix tells you, to the minute, at what time you can eat on every train where eating is possible. Suppose you are going from Paris to Granville and want to lunch in the second sitting. You can eat from 12:15 to 13:47, not a minute longer. He has foreseen everything: if, for instance, you are a voyager of the second class and spend more than half an hour in the wagon restaurant between mealtimes, he knows that you will owe the difference between the second- and first-class fare "for the traject unduly effectuated."

Let it not be thought, however, that M. Chaix is hard of heart. Whenever children or dogs are concerned, he strikes a note of tenderness.

In principle (he says) dogs are not admitted in the passenger carriages; but the company will place in special compartments travellers who do not wish to be separated from their dogs. Moreover dogs of modest stature, enclosed in cages, boxes, or baskets, can be kept in the compartments with the assent of their fellow passengers.

I find many evidences of M. Chaix being a family man, for he is specially kindly toward *Nombreuses Familles*. A Family Ticket of Going and Returning, he tells us, may be had when there travels with the parents a son of less than twenty-one or a daughter of less than twenty-five, and this ticket may also include "the ascendants of this infant; its celibate brothers and sisters of whatever age; two domestics (a male or female cook, a valet or chambermaid or infant's nurse) and if necessary a wet nurse." Below the age of three, he continues, infants pay nothing, on the condition that they are carried on the knees of their family. And among the baggages that may be taken in your compartment with you, he allows babies' bathtubs.

M. Chaix does his best to instil a spirit of foresight and prudence into his flock. I don't suppose any one, in the history of travel, ever followed his instructions for getting a carriage on arrival in Paris. This is what he wants you to do:

Address, 48 hours beforehand, either a letter or a telegram to the Special Carriage Bureau indicating the station and hour of arrival, the number of voyagers, the destination, and the type of carriage desired, whether automotive or of animal traction.

If you want to reserve a berth in a sleeper, M. Chaix urges you to go even more cautiously about it.

The demand for renting a berth must be made at least 4 days in advance; the applicant must deposit, at the same time, as an evidence of good faith, in the hands of the Station Master, a sum of 40 francs. If for any cause the reservations are not utilized on the day and train specified, the totality of the advance payment is definitely acquired by the Administration.

But I think that even M. Chaix feels this to be a bit severe, for he follows by listing the stations where pillows and blankets may be rented by those who find themselves compelled to make overnight journeys not contemplated four days in advance.

If anything goes wrong in your travels, you mustn't blame M. Chaix, for he has told you everything, even down to listing the stations where only passengers without baggages and "dogs with companions" are allowed to board the train. Moreover he urges you not to be content with his work, but to inform yourself further at the office in the Hall of the Lost Feet at the St. Lazare station. Sometimes you feel he is a bit of a dreamer, as when he insists that two children under seven should not occupy more than the space of one adult passenger; sometimes even one suspects him of a gruesome humour, as when he says that a voyager may "renounce an unaccomplished traject" by leaving the train before his destination, provided he also renounces, for the benefit of the administration, the full fare paid for the "uneffectuated totality." Yet certainly he discourages this wanton behaviour, and urges his congregation to be sure that they are not paying more than the stipulated 0.4612 per kilometer for first class, 0.3213 for second, 0.2024 for third.

But I perceive, regretfully, that I haven't given you

any notion of the special delightfulness of M. Chaix. His little time-tables are like any other great charms of life, you have to come upon them for yourself. The real fun of M. Chaix is when you take him from your pocket, in some little provincial train, and with one eye on the scenery and one eye on his tables, begin to figure out your next change. You look for the station marked *B* that means a *buffet* or the *b* that means a *buvette;* you see that the train will wait 30 minutes because it is market day at Paimpol; and that Savigny is a "facultative arrest." Or you may idle over even more exciting sections: how, by writing to Mr. G. S. Szlumper, director of Maritime Services, berths may be had in turbine packetboats between Cherbourg and Southampton; or of return tickets valid from Fat Thursday until Wednesday of the Cinders. For once you learn, with M. Chaix, how easy it really is to travel, you wonder if some day you may not even graduate into his Supreme Work, *The Indicator*—which includes the Grand European Trains Express. In that noble compilation you can work out your "trajects"—not merely in France, but to Rome and Vienna and Petrograd and Constantinople. But for the moment this must be our Facultative Arrest.

A PARIS CROWD

ONE of the delights is that you know no one and
no one knows you. That free and solitary passage
among multitudes can never quite be attained at home;
perhaps only in a foreign city where different language
and different aspect of things turn the mind in upon
itself for its needed reassurance and composure. There
is something divine in the sensation of your secret
swim through this human ocean. You carry your own
heavy and fragile burden of hopes, anxieties, joys, re-
morses, and you know that you will not, from *café
crème* at breakfast to *café cognac* at midnight, encounter any one who has the faintest concern to share
or jostle that curious load. So must the gods have
walked among men. And you marvel at those voyagers
who hasten to inscribe themselves in the register at
the American Express office, to have their names and
hotels chronicled by the *Herald*—in short, who so

readily abandon that most rare and refined of human pleasures, the perfect incognito.

Perhaps the most thrilling crowd in Paris is the crowd in *Père Lachaise*—the crowd of the dead. I wanted specially to see again the monument Aux Morts in its little green ravine. There were some particular graves I should have liked to see, too; but I felt it would be the depth of bad manners to go hunting them out with the aid of a plan. In that perfect democracy of silence only the vulgarest of snobs would be picking and choosing, looking for "famous" tombs. It was a grey drizzling day, the stone-ranked hill was very solitary, and I strolled at random, content (so I found myself rather gruesomely putting it) with the monuments I happened to pass. I will be honest: I had a faint velleity to see the grave of Oscar O'Flaherty Fingalls Wills Wilde (I believe he is buried there) because any man devoted to publishing has a natural interest in the writer who has caused more bogus *de luxe* sets than any other (except perhaps Maupassant?). I wanted to see if the Epstein sphinx which once caused such a row was finally erected. But I didn't find it; and was more than compensated by discovering the tall shaft that the City of Paris has put in memory of her municipal workmen—pipe layers, car conductors, electricians, and others—who have lost their lives in the course of duty.

I don't know (perhaps Sir Thomas Browne or Lord Bacon were the only prowlers who have known) exactly what one feels among these crumblings of mortality. What is our æsthetic of the dust? Is it a small and shamed superiority, to be still topside the gravel? or is it even more disgusting self-pity? At any rate, that noble Aux Morts, unspeakably beautiful tableau of human grief and courage, sends one away with the thoughts "of things that thoughts but tenderly touch." What a thrilling suggestion it gives of our poor final dignity. You see the dying as they approach the end: they come crouching, haggard, stooped in weakness and fear; but at the sill they straighten, shakingly brave, to face that shut door. The man, more sullen or more fearful, still hangs his head. But the woman's face is lifted, and her hand is gently on his shoulder.

If one tries to be honest, he has to be cautious to note where genteel sentiment begins to slide into mere self-concern. After an hour or so of rambling, Père Lachaise begins to weigh on the mind, and crush the purest æsthetic. You are no longer, as the excellent phrase is, disinterested. That congregated mob of the dead is jumbled in an order as rigorously fantastic as names in an index. (Why should the man who invented gas-lighting have so much smaller a tomb than Napoleon's generals who adjoin him? But come to think of it, perhaps his real monument is in Lamb's essays.) You begin to feel an uneasiness, and speculate on the words *Concession à Perpétuité* cut in so many stones. Yes, you say, we must all concede to Perpetuity; but in the meantime, where shall we have lunch? If you feel the pricklings of self-pity, I think it sanative to pause on your way out to look at the grave of de Musset, the enchanting poet and wit who was so gorgeously sorry for himself. He asked to have a

commiserating willow over his tomb; and I noticed that
the growth of the tree has made it necessary to cut
away part of the stone, removing one of his own poems
that he wanted engraved there. There is a kind of
hint in this. More loyal than the willow, his dear old
sister sits chaired in stone just behind him, faithfully
holding a volume of his poems in her lap.

The preceding paragraphs were written three weeks
ago, and have been lying here on the table. If the
two merry little chambermaids of the Hotel G——
could read English—as I know they can't—I wonder
what they would make of them? But perhaps chambermaids in the Latin Quarter are too sagacious to rati-
ocinate about the guests. They sit in their little pantry
at the foot of the stairs and chirp like canaries; and
when you come in, both run out (some day some social
scientist will explain why French chambermaids always
move in pairs), exclaiming excitedly that there was a
telephone call from "The Lady at the Ritz." I wish
that the best of life were not so inenarrably humorous!
I should like to tell you how two telephone calls (you
must take my word for it that the incident was excellently innocent) vastly improved my status at the tiny
Hotel G——.

But I'm glad the earlier sheets lay unmailed, because
my notes on the sense of secret solitude in Paris require
supplement. They were written when my wandering
had been done mostly in the old streets of the Left Side.
I have learned since, pleasantly enough, that along the
Avenue de l'Opéra or the Rue de Rivoli one is certain
to encounter friends from home. That peculiarly in-

timate feeling of utter anonymity is very real and precious, but like all human sensations it quickly passes into a new phase. Apart from the chance tangency with friends, whom one may welcome either for merriment or for advice, it is remarkable how quickly the transplanted life puts out its new fibres, makes its unconscious adhesions, begins to think of the old women in the newspaper-kiosk or the man behind the coffee-bar as its natural associates. It is not far wrong to say that two of the most amazing phenomena in Paris are the number of Americans in the region of the Opera, and the number of Chinamen along the Boule' Mich'. For the latter phenomenon I have no explanation, unless they have fled the chop suey restaurants of Upper Broadway. My friend the Old Mandarin (who is here, too) notes that these young Celestials wear the biggest and broadest-brimmed of the black hats, that they talk French fluently, and are greatly esteemed by the girls of the Latin Quarter. Certainly there are enough handsome women in the world to go round, and I am the last to complain: yet some faint residual shred of race instinct causes me a mild surprise when I see a merry young Chinaman with a smart French damsel on each arm. Coming from America, the land of vehement taboos, one is greatly struck by the Parisian freedom from the cruder forms of prejudice. They really seem to dislike no one but their own politicians.

But it is a city, I still feel, uneasy in its inward heart. The statue of the boy offering masks for sale, in the Luxembourg Gardens, is rather symbolic. In his string of faces there is not one that is tragic. Doesn't that contradict your notion, a friend says, that Paris is anxious inside?

I don't think so. What is the purpose of a laughing mask?

BUSSES AND TRAMS

I'VE been cleaning out my pockets, and have thrown
away a large collection of the little coloured slips
they give you on the busses and trams. The first
week I was in Paris I was too timid to go anywhere
except in taxis. After that I was more timid still. I
understand perfectly how the Marne was won by Paris
taxicabs: they have more *élan* than any other vehicles
in the world. This last fortnight I've travelled widely
in the busses and trolleys, and after a good deal of bash-
ful experiment I've learned their great secret. It happened that every day for two weeks I had to go out
to the leafy suburb of Neuilly, where men sit along the
river fishing for sardines. The French passion for
angling for very small fish is necessitated, I dare say,
by the constant demand for *hors d'œuvres*. Every
morning I took the same bus at the same corner; to be
sure of doing nothing wrong I always sat in the same

seat and got off at the same place. Yet, always asking the conductor how much I should pay, the fare varied daily. Sometimes as low as sixty centimes, sometimes it ran up to ninety, and oscillated among all the sous between. It was as exciting as following the variations of the franc. Then I learned the etiquette. The conductor takes whatever sum you give him and is content. I struck an average between high and low for the ride from the Panthéon to Champerret. Seventy-five centimes, I concluded, was par. Now I give that amount to the conductor and he seems perfectly happy.

In the trams the same method works. But the problem is even more complicated there, because there are more compartments in which you can ride, and they give you a large assortment of coloured slips. If you want to stand in the middle of the car, where you can smoke, you must be specially careful. When the place gets crowded, and (trying to be polite) you shove over a bit to give someone more room, you may be pursued by the conductor, who will ask you for another sou and hand you a little ticket—"Supplement for a Voyager Who Has Transferred Himself from Second Class to First." One day I incautiously allowed myself to get manœuvred on to the front platform, near the motor-man. It was delightful, I smoked and enjoyed the ride; but meanwhile the car had filled up behind me. I saw my destination approaching and began to work my way back toward the only exit, at the rear. But to do so I had to pass through various sections, and in each one someone took away a sou for transferring myself from one class to another.

Busses and Trams

I find it harder and harder to know where literature ends and life begins. There was a very interesting remark in an article on Conrad in the *Journal des Débats* the other day; an article by Joseph Aynard, one of the most penetrating comments on Conrad's work that I have seen. "The more a writer has lived," said M. Aynard, "the more his experience has been enriched, provided only that he has not written too much. For experience itself may be deformed by the desire to write about it." But to keep in touch with *belles lettres* I will say that on tram 35 I saw a man reading Frederick Niven's "Justice of the Peace." I was eager to speak to him and tell him I am a faithful adherent of that fine novel; but I reflected that I had no right to alarm him with my private and irrelevant excitements. I followed him half way round the Madeleine, as a kind of tribute, trying to make up my mind as to his nationality. He looked like a Frenchman who had had a Scotch grandmother; he had a little ribbon decoration in his lapel.

Riding in busses and trams does at any rate give one a great deal of the raw material of literature. Literature I once tried to define for myself as an attempt to make life stand still long enough to be looked at. But life must be looked at without its knowing it is being looked at; and the only way to make it seem to stand still is to travel at exactly the same pace it is travelling. I believe that in the trams, where I have seen women suckling babies and young girls promptly giving up their seats to *mutilés de la guerre*, one may pass a little more truly into the bloodstream of Paris than by sitting on a cane chair, with an *apéritif* and a blue syphon, dreaming at the pavement. Besides, those silvered globes that hold the napkins are too hypnotic, they put you into a trance. There is a jovial story— perhaps it hasn't been written yet—of an American who pursued a rum omelet round the restaurants of Paris. He had somehow heard of this noble dish and had imagined it as the final blaze and brightness in the realm of food: a confection of whipped phœnix eggs bathed in blue flame. But perhaps because his accent was gross, perhaps because he only knew of the thing as "burning eggs," he never could get it. When he asked for it his waiter would call the head waiter, the head waiter would call the *patron*, and they would confer in perplexity with the woman in the *caisse*. Eventually they would bring him a ham sandwich. But one night, at a restaurant by the Chatelet, the *garçon* understood him. The burning omelet was brought, and he singed his moustache in his haste. But instead of the light and tingling texture he had imagined, a dish combining heat and sweetness and savoury nourishment, the expiring flame yawned over a sort of eau-de-cologne syrup, and the yellow mass underneath was cool and fleshy. The only part of the omelet that was really valuable was the allegory; which he afterward pondered as he used to sit at supper in the little Place de la Sorbonne.

Riding in busses and trams is a part of that immensely valuable process of learning the mechanics of a civilization. The great people of the earth don't have to worry about these things, their credit is good anywhere, taxis and couriers and housekeepers are always waiting. But

the little people have to study the details. How to get
a good meal *à prix fixe,* how to move promptly and
cheaply from one point to another, how to mail a *pneu-
matique,* how to get two seats next the windows in a
second-class compartment, how to get a check cashed,
how to take a bath in a small hotel where there's only
one bathroom (and if you slip into the bath without
warning any one the pretty chambermaid comes
pounding on the door with unintelligible and most irregular verbs)—these exhilarating minutiæ are a lively
part of the huge comedy. Riding on the back platform
of a bus you have gorgeous opportunity for study.
You see, in the names of streets and shops, how deeply
a sense of fancy—a literary sense, if you like—is in-
grained in French character. Think of a tiny toy store
called *Aux Délices de l' Age d' Or;* or of the Street of the
Frankly Bourgeois, or the Street of the Bad Boys. You
see those quaint reverses and reciprocations by which
one civilization doffs its hat to another: what *we* call
(on Amsterdam Avenue) a French laundry is here,
always, an American laundry; and goldenrod is sold
on the streets as a rare and precious bloom. One
thing, however, no one can learn: why do they mark
the doors of bookshops *Entrée Libre?* Are there any
bookstores that charge admission?

Even if there were, I fear I should be among the
patrons. My dream of adventure would be to go into
the shop of the Presses Universitaires, on the Boule'
Mich', with an empty suitcase and a bundle of the crisp
blue and yellow hundred-franc notes; to fill the bag with
new, ink-smelling paper-bound books; hop a taxi for

(say) the Gare de Lyon, and in a first-class padded compartment (so like a padded cell) ride all day toward Marseilles or Geneva, reading and wondering. One of the first books I should choose would be one they have in the window—"Esquisse d'Une Philosophie de la Dignité Humaine," written by a Belgian professor. A day so spent would produce madness, but it would be a noble end. But the publishers have added a new terror to death. Nowadays, after an author dies, they hire someone to carry on his characters through new books. They have done that with Pollyanna.

It is chiefly in the emergencies of life that you discover what literature is really most helpful. Suppose you are reading to someone in a hospital, would you choose "Ulysses"? I doubt it. I want to pay a word of tribute, years overdue, to a great master of fiction who has never been touted by the Intellectuals; who is certainly as great a magician of pure plot as O. Henry, and whose humour is less marred by temporary and local allusion. Other writers, no greater, have been reissued in *de luxe* editions with resounding prefaces. When will some publisher do what should be done for W. W. Jacobs? I am interested to see they are beginning to translate him into French.

JULIE

THIS is Julie's afternoon off. At three o'clock the old coachman, with curly white moustaches, clicks the latch of the garden gate. Julie is ready, in her best black apron and the black felt slippers. Her mysterious little packages, treasures accumulated during the past four weeks, are handed up to Monsieur Lecellier with the warning that they are *bien fragiles*. A hat that Titania has given her; some bits of barley sugar and a baby's dress—for the children of her six nephews who own a fishing smack in common; the chintz-covered bottom of a broken trunk tray that has greatly taken her fancy, and the elephant teapot (with his trunk for spout) that Monsieur and Madame brought her from Paris. These, and other small increments, she asks me to inspect, so that I may be assured nothing is exported that does not belong to her. I have tried to persuade Julie it is not necessary to ask our permission every time she wants to eat anything. Accustomed to the manners of American servants, the first time Julie asked if I would permit her to take "a morsel of bread with some butter," I thought it was irony. But far from it. Julie cannot eat or drink with relish until she has had specific assent from above for every item. She used to bring her plate into the dining room, asking me to put her food on it for her. But I suppose we have debauched her by our constant cry, "*Toujours, Julie, vous prendrez tout ce qu'il vous faut.*"

The hat that Julie is taking with her will go, presumably, to one of her grand-nieces; for Julie, when she wears anything on her head, carries the white linen coiffe of the region. The elephant teapot, I surmise, will lead a carefully guarded life. "*Voici, Julie,*" said Monsieur and Madame, "*c'est un peu symbolique, cela servira pour vous faire penser de la famille américaine qui était comme un éléphant sur vos mains.*" But it is always dangerous to touch the sentimental note with Julie, to hint at possible partings. With sudden wetness in her fierce blue eyes she vows that she would not dream of *using* her elephant teapot. "It's sacred," she says. "It's going in a little corner that I know of." To ease the moment one has rapid recourse to stratagem. "*Dans les soirs d'hiver, Julie, vous pourrez prendre votre tilleul dans l'éléphant.*" Julie knows that when *tilleul* is mentioned it is the signal for a laugh. *Tilleul*, a kind of tea made of lime leaves, is her favourite infusion. It smells and tastes like a fragrant hayloft in summer, and she recommends it for every bodily weakness. Monsieur, however, mocks himself of it. Never mind, she says; in fifteen years you will be glad to have recourse to that good *tilleul*.

She climbs into the carriage, gasping a little as she balances on one foot, and drives proudly away to town, to see her two older sisters and tell the latest news of her strange American *patrons*. Only once a month can Julie be persuaded to take a couple of hours off, and then chiefly because she has to visit her *propriétaire*, to pay the rent of "the little corner she knows of." Her wages mustn't be given her until she is all ready to embark; she might lose them. The small black purse is firmly gripped in that strong, laborious hand. Her fine golden-gray head is grandly erect as Monsieur Lecellier drives to town. Life is rich in comely humours, and it happens that Lecellier is her next-door neighbour in the Rue St. Jean. And to be driven up that cobbled lane, arriving in triumph with her bundles, must be good medicine for many days of distress in a long, hard life. What fun it would be, did manners permit, to follow her and see exactly what happens.

In two hours Julie will be back, and come hurrying over to the nearby *chaumière* (forgetting, in her innocent eagerness, that it is forbidden ground: *c'est là que Monsieur écrit son livre*). She is anxious to see if Monsieur and Madame are still alive and well after two dangerous hours unmastiffed; and to report that her sister has sent a present of three pots of jelly. "*Ce pauvre Monsieur! Il n'a jamais assez de confiture.*"

The Romany Stain

How can I tell you about Julie? It cannot be done. But since we live by attempting the impossible, I can take a few symptoms of her vivid human decency. Where shall we begin, then? At the very bottom, with her feet.

It is the sound of those valiant feet, their busy shuffle to and fro, that I think of most affectionately. Toward the middle of the afternoon, when the white canvas sandals are discarded for the soft felt slippers, Julie's feet begin to play an important part in the household. An occasional groan is heard. Then it is not amiss to suggest: Julie, you had better repose yourself a few minutes and drink a little *tilleul*. This has to be said rapidly, round the corner of the door, or Julie may want to show them to you. Once I didn't get away fast enough (it is amazing how rapidly she can get started on a conversation) and there they were. "*Ce sont bien propres*," she exclaimed; and indeed they were like ivory. How that does good, she rejoiced, treading them about on the cold stone flags. When one has sixty-four (years, she means) one has *mal aux pieds*. But unless you daily suggest it, Julie will not repose herself even for five minutes. From before six in the morning until after ten at night, those faithful members are on the go. Perhaps it is along the garden paths, where her fury of washing covers every rosebush with blanching linen; perhaps it is on the road to the farm round the corner, where on muddy days her sabots go clopping for eggs and milk.

Let's try the other end of the picture. Julie is a champion talker. She loves noise. Doors close like artillery; plates come down on the table with a crash. Anything done silently rather frightens her: if you open the kitchen door without preliminary voice or footfall, she whoops with alarm. When our tiny *salle à manger* is packed for *déjeuner*—Monsieur and Madame, three children and Mademoiselle—the din is unbelievable. Every dish is placed with commentary and suggestion. Sometimes Julie tries heroically to restrain herself, for occasionally she has a faint surmise that Madame would relish a little less clamour; but then she hears something said (in our atrocious French) that interests her. She puts her adorable old head on one side, lays a finger against her nose, and waits—with all the excitement of a pleading dog—to catch my eye. This rogueish gesture is irresistible. I look up (if I didn't she would leave the room in tears) and she begins to volley foghorns of talk. At last Titania finds an opportunity to ask for the spoons. *"Ah, je vous fais mal de service!"* the good creature exclaims, conscience-smitten. We all hold our breaths, thinking now we are settled for a moment. But the Urchiness takes this opportunity to try a few words of French, and Julie bursts into a shout of applause. *"Ah, qu'elle est jolie, ma petite cocotte adorée, ah qu'elle est mignonne!"* Titania knows, wisely enough, that Julie is not one of those who can be compressed into the rigid mould of conventional domestic service. I only wish it were possible, without offence, to reproduce some of her more excellent ejaculations—on the virtues of stewed figs or (anatomically gestured, on her own person) the dangers of bicycle riding.

The Romany Stain

How happy an artist would be if he could get Julie
on canvas. He'd have to do it while she's shelling the
beans outside the kitchen door, almost the only time
she could hold a pose. Though I'd like to have her as
she's vigorously swinging the lettuce in a little wire
basket, shaking the water from the leaves. Her handsome blonde head is bent forward, her strong white
forearms flash in the sunlight, she rocks a little on her
big haunches. I hope I haven't given an impression
of a humble, respectful creature: Julie is a true Norman
sea wife, with the stubborn pride and thrift of a rocky
coast and the sea wife's horror of storms. "*Fermez
bien les portes*," is her last cry every night as she toils
up to the attic. "*Nous aurons du vent. Un triste
temps!*" In spite of her horror of frogs (they come
hopping into the house every evening, from the garden)
she will go out to pick pears in the dark and sit late to
cook them, having heard a chance remark that stewed
pears would be nice for breakfast. Her merciless tirade
can be heard a hundred yards down the road if she
imagines that the *épicier* has not given Madame his
best and at the lowest price. Yet a word of reproach
can fill her with black despair. She is one of those who
will suffer anything for love but not raise a hand for
coercion.

One who has always known England much better
than France finds it specially interesting to see these
Norman types so akin to the English in form and spirit.
In the very look of their villages one seems to see the
knotty cradle from which so much of England sprang.

PETITES ANNONCES

THERE is inexhaustible fascination in standing in the corridor of a French *rapide*. The railing is exactly the right height to receive one's elbows, the wide windows give a full view, no official ever dreams of enforcing the notice that "*MM. les Voyageurs* are insistently besought not to sojourn in the aisle." So one can smoke and ponder, not much disturbed until the little waitress with smartly rouged cheeks comes tingling the bell for luncheon, and starts a file of customers along the narrow passage.

And what a serene pattern of landscape. The fields are striped in silver, green, lemon-yellow or a dull glowing gold in sudden shots of sun; and these various oblongs are stitched together with hedges that seem (as swift movement rocks you into a watchful doze) to hold the whole world together in a mesh. Sprinkles of poppies, stubble combed and trimmed, lines of poplars by slow rivers, tawny roofs of tile rich in latent colour as a ripe Stilton cheese. They are long, low, stooping roofs, sagged with burden like a donkey's back, but still strong to endure. A woman in a blue dress, bent over her sickle, pauses to watch the train run by.

But the "omnibus" train—or as we would say, accommodation—is even more fun. It is an easy-going caravan; most of the way you are quite likely to have your second-class compartment to yourself; and when lunch time comes you hop out and buy sandwiches, brioches, pears, and a bottle of white wine (with the cork already loosened for you) at a station buffet. I don't quite know how to work Literature into these dispatches: Doctor Canby writes me that I might say something about what people are reading in France: but Literature, at any rate as boiled down and scummed off into little paper bricks, is not much occupying my mind at the moment. If Doctor Canby knew that the Contributing Editor spends his train journeys reading that scurrile journal, *Madame Sans Gêne* (whose short stories are obscene, but as clever as O. Henry for sheer ingenuity), he would certainly dismiss me. But to look at life solely through the refractions of Literature would be as rash as to assess French civilization by the *Petites Annonces* in *Le Sourire*.

Then, when you lay aside your newspapers, and your invaluable Livret-Chaix, you gape out across the wide fields. The russet light of early autumn is on the slopes of stubble, apples are red and heavy in the trees. The tan-and-white cows of Normandy, you notice, spend most of their time lying down: exhausted, perhaps, by the continual demand upon them for the "*Véritable Camembert de Normandie.*" But the cream-coloured cattle of Burgundy—you can't help remembering Europa and her bull—are on their feet much more. There is the same difference of temper among cathedrals. Chartres is a shrine on tiptoe, leaning and climbing aloft; Bourges is a cathedral sedentary, couched everlastingly upon her restful soil.

In the little train from Dreux to Maintenon, the pane was gone from the tiny window between our compartment and the next. A small boy in the other cell discovered this, and was happy thrusting an umbrella through the aperture. Then I surprised him by blowing a puff of tobacco smoke into *his* compartment. We looked at each other through the hole, and I saw that his sailor cap had a ribbon lettered WILSON. I complimented him on this, told him "*Ça porte bonheur,*" and gave him four sous. When he and his mother got off at Ecluzelles, a heavenly hamlet in that Eure valley that is striped so gold and green, he was still talking about it. The *chef de gare* always looks like an admiral in his gold braid. Such a slamming of doors, blowing of whistles, squawking of the absurd departure signal, all the medley of noise, bustle, and miniature importance that the French relish . . . and off we go, *on time*. The fidelity with which even the smallest branch-line trains stick to their schedule puts the Long Island Railroad to shame. They establish a time-table that they know they can keep—and keep it.

The Romany Stain

One who loves Long Island, by the way, is very much at home in all that central plain. From Chartres to Châteaudun and Blois, across rich sweeps of earth, I could easily imagine myself humming in Dame Quickly from, say, Roslyn to Babylon or Bayshore; though the plains of Eure et Loir are lonelier. The spacious emptiness of French landscape is a constant amazement: every inch in that region is under cultivation, yet one sees few hands at work. A curious echo of home is a line of telegraph that goes humming across the country south of Châteaudun. As soon as you see it you recognize something familiar about the shape of the cross-bars and insulators. Yes, the driver says, it was built by the Americans during the war. It goes to Brest, I suppose, and perhaps the name worn by the urchin of Ecluzelles flashed more than once along those copper threads. Beside the road you pass an occasional patch of our Indian corn—not spaced in hills, but all thickly jumbled together, for fodder, I suppose. Yet at the hotel in Châteaudun—which one is quaintly astounded to find owned and run by an American—you can actually order ears of corn for dinner; and though I am no partisan of American dishes when abroad, I must honestly announce it as thrillingly good. Under the very window where I write, corn is put to still another purpose: it grows in the flower garden, among the gay colours of dahlia and zinnia, as a decorative herb, ornamenting an old château. Just so did Ben Franklin, good solid citizen, find himself an aristocrat when he went abroad.

If you are at Châteaudun, you will rise early and go

out along the road toward Courtalain; and by the
1-kilometer stone you will see a field crossed by a low
stone wall. You cannot mistake this wall, for it
sparkles with bits of broken glass in all lively colours:
green, blue, lilac, yellow, and brown. Over this wall,
beyond a vineyard and a valley, you can get your first
profile of an absolutely unspoiled château—not a re-
decorated trap for tourists like Blois, for instance, but
the genuine majesty and cruelty of the Middle Ages.
Happily the castles of the Loire (how can I persuade the
printer, at such distance, to spell this Loire differently
from the earlier one? He will certainly conclude the
calamus has lapsed) have been made such an industry
that most travellers are wearied out before they reach
Châteaudun; and you can enjoy it in lonely peace. The
wise are content to say little of their richest trove: I
have already said too much. I will only add, to assure
Doctor Canby that I am aware of current literature,
that in Châteaudun there is a *coiffeur* called Proust.

A necessary ingredient of any full experience is
terror; I came close to it when M. Battais, one of the
caretakers of Chartres cathedral (to whom I had gone
provided with secret passwords), instructed me to help
him ring the noonday bells. In the roaring cave of
that lacy spire, see-sawing on the crossbeam of a bronze
monster that seemed as maniac as Victor Hugo's can-
non, we sprang and clung. Through the long windows
the sunny roofs of Chartres, far below, spun a fantastic
rigolo. You grasp an iron bar on the fixed rafter above
the great bell. With one foot on the airy scaffold,
you put the other on the rocking crossbeam, and begin

with gently measured shoves. Then, stronger and stronger you bear down, sinking lower each dip as the bronze begins to roll. With a jarring thunder the metal takes voice and comes alive. Farther and farther down you swing, on one foot, until the other leg loses its purchase on the platform. Now, with a wild capering you reel up and down, watching M. Battais in his shirtsleeves and skull cap as he grimly oscillates on the other side. The bell is already making nearly a 180-degree swing; the shaking explosions of sound are bewildering; you begin to wonder if it is his intention to make it go all the way round? For you didn't catch any too clearly just what he had told you, in French, to do next—except to hold on tight. You meditate sadly, as you bound on and off the flying beam, that the spire is centuries old, and that this appalling vibration is enough to burst the silver-grey stones asunder. To-day, to-day evidently, is the final moment when disintegration is due. How startled Titania will be, calmly sitting at the Grand Monarque inn, to hear the crash; and you yourself to be assimilated from fragments of stained glass and lichen. The adorable ironies of life! You came to Chartres, a simple pilgrim, in quest of its solemn peace: and here you ride a mustang bronze, a hundred yards in air, that shouts toward God in a hullabaloo the Seventh Avenue subway never dreamed. Then it is over: you stand wiping your brow among the pinnacles, while M. Battais dislodges a tiny seed pod of yellow gilliflower, growing between the toes of a stone chimera, for you to plant in your garden at home.

Petites Annonces

I'm sorry I didn't see M. Battais's dog, with whom and a big revolver he sleeps at night in his tiny bedroom hidden among the carved screenery around the choir. There must be good sleeping in that little cavern, and when there is a moon—or better still, he assured me, a thunderstorm, with flashes of lightning—one can imagine his instants of glamour. There was a creature at the southwest corner of the cathedral, outside, sitting up on his haunches, who looked like a dog, though he had lost his head. Titania believed him to be our old friend Mr. Gissing. If it were so, he might well have lost his head; for I think he would have found the blue he wanted in the west windows at Chartres . . . the colour that embraces everything from a *Petite Annonce* to the Annunciation.

AN OLD HOUSE IN BURGUNDY

BETWEEN two great rivers that run almost parallel but in opposite directions, there are two hill-ranges, the Morvan and the Côte d'Or. Between these hills there is a tranquil region of upland valleys, rich in ruined castles, where the streams are uncertain whether to decant northward to the Seine, or westward to the Loire, or southeast to the Saône. The cider of Normandy, the yellow wine of Anjou, the purple of Burgundy, here balance as ultimate destiny. It is not only the watershed of France, it is the wineshed. But, however geographers may map it, there is no doubt in the region's own sentiment. It looks toward the Mediterranean and the South. When the Reds of Marseilles marched to Paris, they were nowhere more warmly welcomed than at Saulieu. From the vineyard slopes above Beaune, in clearest weather, Mont Blanc can be seen floating in the sky. So they all say,

at any rate, and so Stendhal and many others have
recorded, though it seems astounding: the peak must
be 125 miles away. I could only see the pink roads
the same dusky pink as the inward staves of a wine-
vat; and the church in Beaune that is the shape of a
bottle. For when you cross that ridge of the Côte d'Or
and come (through a village called Bouze) down vineyard slopes in a hot September sun, you are among
the world's most famous grapes. The rapid opening
and closing of the straight vistas between vine-rows,
as the car spins by, makes the fields change and shimmer
like twinkling silk. As you study the wine card at the
inn at Beaune you can meditate those historic names:
Volnay, Pommard, Corton, Chambertin, Montrachet,
Clos-Vougeot . . . Clos-Vougeot to whom one of
Napoleon's commanders made his regiment present
arms when they marched by. It was another military
man (Camille Rodier's great work on *Le Vin de Bourgogne* tells the story) who always drank his burgundies
in a glass cheese-bell. For it is the Burgundian theory
that wine should be drunk in a vessel large enough to
admit both mouth and nose simultaneously. *"Ce n'est
évidemment pas très élégant, mais une nouvelle série
d'odeurs perçues par les fosses nasales sera le bénéfice,"*
says Camille Rodier. The glasses set out by the inn
at Beaune are not quite as wide as cheese-bells, but
very nearly. I now understand more clearly how it
was that Mr. Hamish Miles three times began a letter
to me, a year ago, when staying at Beaune; and three
times desisted, overcome with sleep. He finished the
letter a month later, in London. It was a powerful

letter, and concluded by quoting the wine card of the hotel, where you will find written: *"Ce n'est pas à dire que l'amateur de Bourgogne soit toujours un homme supérieur, mais c'est un être essentiellement perfectible. C'est un humaniste, sinon en substance, du moins en puissance, car on remarquera presque toujours chez lui un souci d'élégance dans l'expression de la pensée, un amour des bonnes lettres, de l'éloquence ou des arts."*

Yet it was not of wine that I intended to write, but of an old house in Burgundy; an old house lying in that valley just west of the Côte d'Or hills, deep-set in such peaceable calm as only an inland valley can give. I should really call it a château, for such it is; but to the usual American connotation that word is too likely to suggest a place fantastically ornate. I would not mar its perfect sober dignity by a misleading word.

It is curious how hard it is in words to convey the simple serenity of that old house, with its cone-topped towers duplicated in the broad still moat. Nervous and apprehensive as we are, there is something guilty in the way we shrink from describing peace. Dignity and serenity are the words, perhaps. In that roomy building of stone floors and great oaken beams life seems to shine as clear, as rich, as strong, as colour through stained glass or through the dark wines of Aloxe and Savigny that ripen in its cellar. In every plain doorway, in every curve of stone stair or twist of ironwork or slope of mossed tile roof, there is the sense of long tranquillity, decent and friendly and kind. But there is something happier there than mere tranquillity: a feeling of renaissance, of convalescence, as of an old

An Old House in Burgundy

loveliness that had fallen into misery and decay, and now finds itself in hands that can support and reënliven it. At the back of the fireplaces, when the blaze is going, you can see the emblem of former seigneurs: a right hand, lifted open, palm outward. A Glad Hand, we can call it, emblem of a beautiful name, Suremain de Saiserey, which sounds as though it meant something like A Sure Hand to Hold. But the surest hand may relax when there are no heirs to carry on.

Sometimes Americans seem the appointed lovers and custodians of European secrets: there was some strange blessing at work when (armed only with a postcard photo from which the name had been cut off) my friend the Caliph ferreted out this old house—which the owners were prepared to sell piecemeal and where poultry was kept in cages on the big stone stair. Looking across the moat on moonlit evenings, where the shadow of 13th-century towers lay black-pointed on the meadow, there was no sound except the splash of wakeful carp. Sitting by candlelight to study 18th-century vellum-bound account books (there was a cowhide trunk full of old records of the house) or hunting up the story of the romantic young poet who loved the château and ran away from home to fight for Poland and died young; or admiring the portrait of the Duchesse de Foix, in a scarlet gown and green-gold mantle, gaily holding a tiny black mask, one knew the old house to be very much alive.

Who shall explain what miracle it is that happens when a man finds just that angle of earth that smiles particularly for him? In the Caliph's face as he ponders the stone facets of his moat-balustrade, or the hipped gables of his farm buildings, or the curved steps that lead down to his bowling green, or the arch of his alley of lime trees, I see the look of a man at peace with life. Architect by profession, his two or three months a year in this Burgundian retreat are certainly no mere vacancy, but a devotion to the bottom principles and honours of his art; from which he takes back, to his office in an American city, freshened notions of that marriage of Place and Time that we call architecture. And what delightful ironies in the situation, he chuckles. Is it not amusing, he says, that a Scotch-American Presbyterian, brought up to believe (almost) that Papists have horns and hoofs, finds himself seigneur of a Catholic hamlet, with a chapel in his own grounds and a village church under his windows where he must provide for sixty-some masses a year to be performed for his house's ancestors? How is it, he asks, that he feels more at home here than anywhere else in the world— here where he doesn't even understand their language? Like the wise man he is, he says very little to casual acquaintances at home about the house where the welcoming hand shines on the chimneyback. Evasive magic comes to pass when a man's heart takes root, for a few months a year, in a life that is strangely different from his own and yet also strangely blended. It is no mean lesson to have lived, even for a week only, in that old house. One brings away more than memories of licheny stonework rising from a clear mirror of water: a sense that the art of living has sometimes triumphed (and can again) over muddle and dis-

traction; that (as the humorous wine card has it) a
lover of these things might even be "an essentially perfectible being." It will be pleasant for the Caliph to
think sometimes, in the subway, that a cask of Corton
1919 (the same that we sampled, from a silver tasting-
cup, in the dark vaults under a Côte d'Or hillside) is
ripening all the long winter months in the cellar beneath the château. He carries the meaning and destiny
of that old house deep settled in his mind, like a bottle
of good wine.

II

The little river Serein (so I learn from Mr. H. Warner
Allen's book "The Wines of France") divides the vine-
yards of Chablis, so that the vintages of that region are
classified according to whether they ferment on the right
or the left bank. It is the same stream which in its
infancy makes a clear ring round this old château, on
its way toward the Yonne and the Seine.

It is the Serein that idles gently at the foot of this
13th-century stone tower, where a fire burns behind
me, lighting up the open hand cast in the iron chimneyback. Suremain de Flammerans was the name of one
of the old seigneurs, and his emblem still shines hospit-
ably behind the flames. This queer old painted room,
within walls five feet thick, has been unoccupied for
generations. We have sounded all the panellings for
secret slides—not successfully, alas; though the house
has its mysteries, as you shall see. A room with a stone
floor, by the way, is ideal as a study; you can throw your
matches and ashes where you please, and brush them
into the hearth afterward.

The Romany Stain

The little Serein, moving softly in its stony moat, is one of this place's most perfect charms. The wind stirs it in parallel scribbles that move round the walls as softly as unwritten lines of verse drift in a poet's mind. Loitering on the bridge, in a forenoon of Meursault-coloured sunlight, I heard Luther Conradi playing in the music room. The rippling notes came trembling out into the sweet September air: a glorious cascade of trebles, gay and hasty with a downward-running cadence. At once the melody made me think of a little stream slipping and bending on its way; I imagined the Serein and its contributors tinkling down from Burgundian hillsides; and when I asked Conradi what it was, he said Liszt's *Au Bord d'une Source*. A few nights before, he had been playing this composition before going to bed. He woke just before dawn and heard someone in the music room (next his chamber) playing it again. He sat up in bed amazed at the charm and sureness of touch; and then, to his astonishment, the music rippled on to a new and singularly beautiful ending, different from the composer's. In the spell of half-sleep he thought it must be a dream, and lay down again. But the next morning two others, sleeping at opposite ends of the house, said they had heard music during the night. I have heard him play that new ending of the piece as he heard it in the darkness; it is quite different from Liszt's and not less beautiful. It has a curious upward striving, as though the rivulet were trying to flow backward to its unvexed origin.

It is the little Serein, bending round the château, that seems the *motif* of whatever secret music lingers

An Old House in Burgundy

here in unmeasurable vibrations of air. The circle of
water binds it in, sets it delicately apart, isolates it with
such careful artifice. A tiny stream, so easily crossed:
it is really but a few feet of water but its reflections are
so deep! It is a great artist, the Serein: it knows that
the way to savour a great silence is to have just a little
sound; so at night, through open windows, you can hear
it whispering past its overflow; on its way, past meadows
and white cattle, toward larger destinies. Here it is
like the daily mind of man—shallow itself, but it can
mirror the pictures of great things.

Silence is a great part of the life the Serein here en-
closes. A peacefulness so profound that one wants to
retard every slow moment and see it from both sides.
Within and without, an old domain like this is a work
of art, an art so deeply established that it collaborates
with the supreme artfulness of Nature. Nature has the
vague impulse, the push; man merely provides the
rhyme-scheme, the ABBA. In the oddest variety
everything here suggests artistic parables. On a sunny
morning the shadow of this tower falls definite and dark
across the brown moat. The carp, in a thick cluster,
shoal to and fro exactly along the line of that shadow,
keeping to the darker side. Is that not art? When the
church bell rings, or a clock strikes, it seems always to
fall upon the ear exactly at the right moment, at the instant when the apprehensions needed it. The wine
stacked in bins in the cellar, to lie there cool and obscure,
for years to come—the act of placing it has a ritual
gravity. And brought upstairs in its little basket, like
a baby in a bassinette, carefully horizontal, a bottle of

[101]

The Romany Stain

Musigny or Corton-Grancey has the full righteousness
of colour, bouquet, and *goût* that make it as perfect in its
own realm as an ode by Keats. There is no tariff in
these matters. Perfection costs whatever you have to
pay for it. Indeed the exhalation rising from a wine
like Musigny, the ghost of the grape rising in the clear
half-empty crater of those vast goblets, is so divine that it
would seem the supreme act of connoisseurship simply to
relish it in the nostrils and never taste it at all. Nor is it
wise to taste rich Burgundies too continuously; the Sub-
scriber in Waterbury who reproached me for an interest
in such matters may console himself with the linguistic
reflection that *goût* is easily transformed into gout.

I think I had forgotten to tell you about Burgundian
clocks, which are amusing. The nearer one gets to
Switzerland, I have always observed, the more people
are interested in clocks. Perhaps that is because the
Swiss, placed by Nature so near eternity, find earthly
divisions of Time all the more precious. America invented the alarm clock, which rouses man to his work,
and the time clock which keeps him at it. The Burgundian, taking it for granted that a solid citizen is for a
large part of his time engrossed in the distractions of
the table, conceived the idea of a clock that would strike
the hour twice, to make sure of your noticing it correctly. The first time, while you are toping or gossiping,
the clock strikes at random, anything at all, perhaps
exactly, perhaps not. But then, a couple of minutes
later, when your attention has been called to the
fact that another hour has ticked, the number is correctly clanged. Such is a Burgundian clock.

An Old House in Burgundy

But the thought that the Serein and I were pursuing was that everything here seems (as a printer would say) *justified:* aligned and accurately imposed upon some underlying norm. When Conradi was playing the other evening, I sat near to watch his hands: it seemed impossible that they should err. The musician playing a difficult composition, he said, is always singing it in his mind. In the same way, in rare coalitions of circumstance, some subconscious spirit of just and fine living seems to be singing the complicated counterpoint of our existence. With it all, unless I misconceive the spirit of an old house, one is pervaded now and then by a delightful enchanted sadness. But the Serein has its gaieties too; and Conradi and I are meditating a Moating Song—a form of nautical ballad not yet achieved, I think.

Returning to France revives in the poet, who has not written verse for a longish time, an eagerness to put his notions in rhyme. In the train from Granville to Paris, and again from Paris toward Dijon, the measured charm of those countrysides, the reddening orchards, white curly roads, neatly shaven plains and stripy hillsides, silver-grey hamlets and the blue curves of the Yonne and aisles of poplar trees, all seemed to suggest and require the old French forms of verse. In the ballade or rondeau the singer spreads his thoughts with the simple orderliness of a peasant sunning linen on a hedge.

And this evening we are going, quixotically, to tilt some Moulin-à-Vent. As one might write on a picture postcard: We are having an uncorking time.

A LETTER TO HENRY

CHESTERTON once said, my dear Henry, that though the British Empire had discovered almost everything else it had never discovered England. Perhaps indeed it is the Americans—some Americans—who are most likely to discover it: for we bring to it so healthy an appetite for just those viands that are the blood and gravy of English feeling. At home, often, our minds are stuffed rather than fed.

You begin to discover England when you get aboard the boat train at the Gare du Nord. Those voices: how adorably indescriptibly odd to the American ear! It is, seemingly, your own tongue, for (to your surprise, after months in France) you find you can understand the fragments you overhear; yet it is said in the most delicious lifting and softness of intonation. As different from our lingo as English grass from American grass. Then, when you go into the wagon restaurant for a cup of tea, you find that the French (with their divine and erring courtesy) have tried to make their guests at home. There are little pots of marmalade on the tables, and platters of what the Company of Wagon-Lits fondly believes to be toast. And even slices of "plum cake." The other day in Paris a pink-cheeked little English flapper sat next to Titania and me at Smith's tea-room, over the bookshop, Rue de Rivoli, and had a thoroughly girlish snack: ice-cream with buttered toast. Then she called for "A slice of plum cake," and I knew that England wasn't far away. The fields of the Somme were won, not on the playgrounds of Eton, but in the tea-rooms of J. Lyons. You've heard of British Lyons. I can't quite make you understand why that pretty child (her name, I think, was Kathleen) asking for "plum cake" was to me a whole essay on European history.

On the deck of the cross-channel steamer *Riviera*, Boulogne to Folkestone. Is there anything more exciting than seeing, from mid-stream, a dark wet night, the lights of France and England simultaneously? All those lighthouses twinkling away like drugstores on both sides of a wide street. France seems to have the best of it: the light at Gris-Nez is brightest of all. "Do you know, sir," said the charmingly polite English passport officer, questioning me in the smokeroom, "you're positively the first American I've ever met without a middle initial." Only the non-British have to be passported on the boat: there were a few French, several Americans, and a little Jap giggling to everyone with almost hysterical friendliness. The Englishmen were mostly at the bar, ordering "a small Bass."

What a day, my ancient! At 5:30 of a cold rainy morning, coffee on the far western coast of Normandy. At midday, filet of sole and a bottle of Aloxe-Corton with the Caliph at Marguery's in Paris. Passing through Amiens and Abbéville, that dark devastation which the Wagon-Lits stewards deem tea. In the second-class compartment from Folkestone to Victoria, "a small Bass," while I read in an evening paper, with shame, an American playwright's article explaining why he thinks that a million people should see his play, just opened in London. I had Proust's "Les Plaisirs et les Jours" in my pocket, but I can't read real things while travelling in unfamiliar scenes. I am too nervously and miserably happy. At Victoria I was met by a young kinsman who insisted on coffee and liqueurs. Then the 11:30 train to the moist and fragrant darkness of Surrey. Arriving at Effingham, opposite the Plough Inn there is a little old cottage buried among hollyhocks and cabbages. Lovelace once lived there, they tell me. Beer and books were waiting. How does one sleep, at 1:30 A. M., after a day like that? But I found there the latest issue of the *Saturday Review*, and took it to bed, by candlelight, in a tiny cupboard-bedroom where you lie with your feet almost out of the little leaded window. I was just dozing off when I found that your compositor had turned my "inenarrably" into "inerrantly." This made me so peevish it woke me up again. I had to turn to the

A Letter to Henry

editorial, dealing, as usual, with the Future of American Literature.

When I woke up, the soft September drizzle was pearling the hollyhocks and cabbages. It's lucky, by the way, that Yorkshire pudding doesn't grow on a bush: one would be given it at every meal. But this was my first morning in England for eleven years, my Henry; and I was going to have bacon and tea. I often wondered why Edna Ferber went out of her way to poop off at English bacon in "So Big." I don't think she knows what she's talking about. Another matter that pleased me, I meant to mention it before, I was reading David Garnett's "Man in the Zoo" in bed in the hotel in Cherbourg, last June, when I found him mentioning "Cooper's Oxford Marmalade." I knew then that it was a good book. Garnett and the Bowling Green, I think, are the only two attempts to get Cooper's Marmalade into literature.

A little later I was in a taxi, on my way to Cavendish Square. I passed some park or other—let's say it was St. James's: I haven't yet recovered my London geography—and something hit me, so hard that I felt ill in my bowels. It was my love for London. I know that good manners impel one to apologize for loving things. What I'm getting at, old magistrate, is this: don't worry too much about the Future of American Literature. It will come along all right, as any kind of art comes along, when we love things enough. Which doesn't mean blurbing about them, but trying to enter into their secret perils and meanings. And as that dear man H. M. Tomlinson says, when you talk to him about these matters and his face lights up vaguely and he murmurs the rich prose of his mind in a soft crooning whisper, "My God," he says, "you've had Whitman and Melville and Thoreau and Emily Dickinson. Isn't that enough for a century or so?"

When we love things with the terrible shuddering love of Emily Dickinson for her Amherst garden, for instance, literature happens—or else silence. There are a lot of dangerously smart people turning out the New Palaver on our side, with tongue in both cheeks at once. George Gissing would say that we haven't starved enough. I should say we haven't yearned quite enough.

But London, I repeat (you must allow a little lunacy to one coming back after eleven wild years) makes me wamble with love and terror. Paris, divine though she is, seems to fade out and grow dim. Is it because London is so much less eloquent that she seems to have much more to say? That is literally it; and it is the unsaid things that concern literature. You know the type of Englishman who means most to our hearts: the man with whom it is difficult to communicate, but easy to commune.

And one of the loveliest things about London is, she brings me so much nearer to New York—the only city where I find my own dangerous peace. My heart is blithe to think of our polyglot skyline of insanity. And with all our sins, we have never quite been complacent about her, as some of our friends here are complacent about the London we love as much as they.

All this, you see, has been for me not discovery but

A Letter to Henry

verification. It is strangely mixed up with thoughts of a man who really did discover England, and as I came through Kent in the dark I thought how much poorer England is since he sailed. Of course, I mean Conrad. It is strange to think of the incredible wealth of that mind, its memories and brooded insights upon men, its nobly just division of love and scorn, its lonely affectionate simpleness, lost to us for always. Even his gravestone, they tell me, carries his Polish name. When the English think about Conrad, it will make them very generous toward "foreigners"—even to Americans, who have not the charm of real foreigners. But they are already more generous to us than we deserve.

I was passing by the Museum Tavern—opposite the British Museum—just as they unbarred the door for the noon opening (it is Sunday). I went in, and drinking a tall one of shandygaff and admiring a pink section of ham and a vast slab of cheese (there's something rather good about ham in Amy Lowell's poem about England) which would have done you good to consider, I pondered how to write to you as you deserve. Don't let the too-easy critics wear out their fingers pointing to the scenery, as the excellent phrase is. Literature comes where and when you're not looking for it. Some day, just as some strange shabby bird is passing by, the pub door of Helicon will be unbarred and a Ganymede in shirtsleeves with foam on his moustache will beckon him in.

REWARDS—AND FAIRIES

THE Manchester *Guardian's* London correspondent
tells a story of a young officer commanding a
machine-gun outpost. He was cut off from his own
lines in one of the German pushes, and the last words
that came over the 'phone were: "All done in except
the sergeant and me. Four rounds of ammunition
left, but the gun's jammed. Don't expect anything
showy."

You won't expect anything showy from the Green
in regard to its brief adventures in England. Particularly not from this quiet room in King's Bench
Walk. I sit in a friend's chambers in the Inner Temple,
looking out toward the winged horse on the spire of the
Hall. My host himself, one of a family whose genius
consists of intuition without exclamation, is a master
of shrewd statement—not so much understatement

as innerstatement. I don't know whether you saw his description (in the *Guardian*) of Conrad's funeral: of the strange feelings caused by the cortège which moved through a town dripping with flags (it was Canterbury's annual festival week) so that the colours J. C. had honoured almost touched the hearse as it passed; and how the coffin was lowered into clean whiteness, the graveyard being on Kentish chalk. Those are the things that my host sees, and sends nightly over the wire to Manchester, to the paper that many of us have always believed one of the few really great journals.

So the courts and buildings of the Temple justly move one toward a decency of thrifty words. There is nothing showy about the stone behind the church with the plain words "Here lies Oliver Goldsmith." The porter with his top hat, the under porter in his brown and yellow robe, are perhaps a little more spectacular, but they have their dignity too. In the building where Lamb was born there is a broken window pane, which report ascribes to some humourist with a pea-shooter who besieged Sinclair Lewis there when Lewis was working on "Martin Arrowsmith." Perhaps the pane has been left unmended as a delicate tribute to American literature. That would be like the Temple's gracious and humorous ways. The only accent of doubt that I have heard was in the gently questioning voice of H. M. T., with whom I went prowling an afternoon. We visited All Hallows, Barking (a church where Mr. Gissing would have gladly been lay reader), and admired the Thames-side pubs and warehouses of Wapping and Stepney. We couldn't enter the Turk's Head (run by a Mr. Gulliver) or the Town of Ramsgate or other famous inns, as they are closed in the afternoon; but we poked about the old docks where Conrad used to tie up; and then H. M. T. said suddenly, "What does one of your professors mean when he says Miss So-and-so's books 'reek with cerebration'?"

Perhaps the best thing written about England lately is Karel Capek's delicious series of articles in—yes, again—the Manchester *Guardian*, called "How It Feels to Be in England." Capek, of course, has the advantage of being a real foreigner; what, among us, would be esteemed too lavish sentiment, seems in a foreign voice delightful, subtle naïveté. At any rate, he has put down, and illustrated with quaint drawings, the soft disturbances of his mind, the things we all feel—such as the beauty of London policemen, the honourable silence of club rooms, the domed shrubbiness of English trees, the strongly satisfying bulk of English food. These thrillingly perceptive memoranda of his will surely (I hope) be published in book form, for we cannot have too much of that sort of thing. Most visitors succumb to the comfortable grace of England and accept it; but Capek, with the poet's trouble in his mind, has tried to peer into that grace and see that she is enchanting because she is really bewitched. Here more than anywhere, I suppose, it was really doubtful whether men or fairies should have empire. By this time, some of the elves have been smoked out, yet I saw two goblins last night—two little misshapen

costers, a man and a woman, dancing in the Strand.
The man in his tweed cap, the girl, a lumpish bundle
of skirts, footed it on the pavement in a kind of fiercely
solemn reel, and no one seemed to pay any heed. And
on a dockbridge in Wapping we saw a group of old
Jewish women gathered about a still older one who was
reading some Oriental scriptures aloud. She droned
and keened in a wailing chant, an ecstasy of despair;
the others huddled round her and wiped their eyes as
they listened. The scene of merriment, the scene of
penance, both were invasions from some strange world
I have not known and can never know—which is what
I mean by fairyland. And why, if not to put the fear
of the good old English God into the hearts of the
fairies, should the Strand churchbells make strange
jangle toward twilight on Sundays? There is no one on
Fleet Street then but newspaper men; and newspaper
men and elves have much in common. It was a
newspaper man who left the back door open (in Ken-
sington Gardens) and allowed so many of the fey people
to slip in again.

The emblem of strange magic is upon so many things
in England. You go to St. Pancras to take a train
for Manchester, and you find a beautiful crimson
locomotive on which are painted a thistle, a rose and
a dragon's wing. You go sailing on the Thames, in a
dinghy, between Chiswick and Barnes, and in the
tawny sunsets (sunsets in London, like port wine, are
of two kinds: the *tawny* and the *ruby*) a factory chimney
is sending up a plume of lavender-coloured smoke.
And in Manchester itself, there is a man who polishes

the brass nameplate of a big clothing store—or should I say a "draper's shop"? He has moustaches that spike out six inches on each side, gummed and stiffened so that birds could perch on them. He will tell you, if you admire the clothing dummy in the window, that it was modelled after Carpenteer, the Frenchman, and cost a hundred guineas. (I wonder if Georges draws a royalty on his effigies that are so popular in shop windows?) And there is the waiter at the Cheshire Cheese, who brings you a platter saying, "This is our lark pie, sir." On its back in the platter is a bird lying decently stark, its claws curled up and hooked in its beak. It seems a rather large and gaudy lark, you think—a skylark stained by a Wapping sunset, perhaps—and then you see the creature's dark ink-drop eye ribaldly conning you. It is the Cheese's famous parrot: he has been there thirty-eight years, and this is one of his tricks. The same fowl, on Armistice Night, roused to frenzy by the celebration, repeated three hundred times his imitation of a cork being pulled, and fell in a swoon.

Of course, I have not proved it (it cannot be proved) but it seems plain to me that in England the fairies put up a grand struggle before they were beaten; and they have left their mark on their conquerors. A man who has fought with them has strange carvings on his face. I saw Dean Inge, for instance, cutting the steak pudding by candlelight, the night the Pudding Season opened at the Cheshire Cheese. He had a delightfully wry smile as the flashlights kept popping off—the Cheese takes good care that these events get into the illustrated papers—as though some Puck was telling him that Doctor Johnson would have been sorry to find the Cheese so keen for publicity. "Ye oldë flashlyghtë and ye oldë electrick fan," Mr. Muirhead Bone kept humorously exclaiming as he noted these features of the ancient inn.

England expects every American to do his duty: which is to see, and exult in, those miraculous accidents of beauty that have made her life so precious. To read the names and addresses in the visitors' book at the Cheshire Cheese, will show you how loyally our docible countrymen obey. But often we find the things that are loveliest flashlit by sudden blazes of innocent irony. It is the fairies who do this: it is their last revenge.

Perhaps, after all, they haven't really been beaten. I saw Sir James Barrie's windows lighted above Adelphi Terrace last night: how I should have liked to ask *him*. Certainly, twice, riding in taxies, the driver forgot to start his meter until we were halfway there: that never happened to me before, and argues magic. And in Brixton there is a wine merchant (you can verify this in the London 'phone book) whose name is Christopher Morley.

A MAP OF LONDON

I

I'VE just been looking at the map, my precious old
map of London which I bought a fine, dark, drizzling
evening in November, 1910, at a little shop in Praed
Street, near Paddington Station. It's not likely that I
shall forget that evening: it was my first foray into
London on my own, and perhaps it was all the more
cherishable because the liberty was only momentary:
for I had to catch the 9:50 back to Oxford—the famous
train (if I remember accurately) which was the latest
one could take to be back in college before midnight.
(Doesn't one still hear those Oxford hansoms jingling
through the dark, clashing round the narrow angles of
New College Lane?) So I can plainly see Praed Street
in foggy darkness, shop windows bright with invitation,
and a gigantic commissionaire in uniform outside the
door of some music hall or vaudeville theatre (or could

it have been a movie?). And all these intervening
years my map, stoutly backed with muslin and with
an ingenious mensurated tape for finding any desired
street by an index-number, has been waiting on the
bookshelf. It was the first thing I put into my trunk
when I came abroad last spring. What fun I would
have (I promised myself) re-exploring the scenes of
youthful wanders. And then (how delightfully ironical is plain fact) when I actually found myself in London
I never had time to open it—except once, hastily, to
verify the exact topography of that central trapezoid
which is the nub of visitor's London. Oxford Street,
Regent Street, Haymarket, Kingsway, and Strand—
X'd, like a pair of firemen's suspenders, by Shaftesbury
Avenue and Charing Cross Road.

And now, London being again nothing but a dream,
I get out the map and mumble a bit to myself over the
places I meant to look at and didn't. I find that I
can't even remember the meanings of marks I put on
it fourteen years ago. I find a black circle round St.
Stephen's Square, Bayswater: I savvy that all right,
that's where Elmer Keith and I had lodgings at Christmas, 1910, so cold that we slept in swathes of the
Times (with the *Literary Supplement* as foot-warmers).
And I know what this mark means on Guilford Street,
W. C., the most momentous address of my life. But
what is this carefully inked blob on Lansdowne Cres-
cent? Did anything exciting happen to me there? I
haven't the faintest recollection of it.

What I really got out the map for was to see exactly
where is Bessborough Gardens, which I meant to visit

The Romany Stain

and didn't. In "A Personal Record," I think, Conrad
told us that it was there, in lodgings, that his career as a
writer began, while he was waiting for the landlady's
daughter to clear away the breakfast tray.   And I can
understand the scene perfectly: for it is after breakfast
in London lodgings, after tea and bacon and toast, to
be precise, when you are lighting your pipe and warming the slack of your breeks at a minuscule warmth of
coals, that one can feel most easily the flowing movement of mind that presages authorship.   I hunt out
Bessborough Gardens on the map and find it only a
little way from the Tate Gallery (where Epstein's bust
of Conrad now is) just above Vauxhall Bridge.   It
is an offshoot of Lupus Street, just the place where a
man might begin writing to keep the wolf from the
door.   Why didn't I have time to see Lupus Street?

Yet certainly I am not going to brood upon things
I didn't reach, when I saw so much more than I de-
served or expected.   I wish I could remember the name
of the genial old hotel (was it in the Commercial Road?
or perhaps nearer Aldgate?) that H. M. Tomlinson
pointed out to me as a traditional resort of sea-captains.
For my own part, I discovered what is not too common
in Europe, a comfortable little hotel with not a single
American in it but myself, nor did I even see the names
of any in the register.   There was a parson there with
gaiters and an apron: he may even have been a Bishop
("solemnly pursuing his bird," if you remember your
"Trivia") or he may have been, like the ecclesiast in
Elizabeth's "In the Mountains," someone who expected soon to be a Bishop ("*Il n'est pas un évêque mais*

[118]

A Map of London

il est presque un"). When he entered the breakfast room and ordered haddock and grilled kidneys and bacon, and unfolded his *Times* (naturally a solemnifying rite, as it is the Deaths and Marriages that one sees first; and you can't get to be a Bishop without knowing all sorts of people who are likely to be dead) the scene was as English as Runnymede. For England is different from other countries in that it really *is* exactly as it has been described. I have only one fraud to report, and that is the "mahogany tree" that Thackeray wrote about—the table in the *Punch* office where the thirteen lucky editors sit down for their weekly staff dinner. The board was already laid, with plenty of wine glasses, when I was there, but Ewan Agnew lifted the cloth—and it isn't mahogany at all, but a fine old slab of soft deal. If it had been mahogany probably they wouldn't all have carved their initials in it. W. M. T. and E. V. L. are the best carved monograms in the lot. Mark Twain, I believe, remains the only visitor who has dined with the staff: I wonder if they asked him to cut his initials in the board? Certainly he would have enjoyed doing so. Or perhaps he would have said that two thirds of Thackeray's would be enough for him.

The pubs, as you probably know, shut down at 10:30 in the evening: one wonders what Doctor Johnson would have thought of being ejected from the Cheshire Cheese at that hour? Along Fleet Street one sees none of the all-night lunchrooms that cheer the heart of the late journalist in American cities. The only recourse at that hour is to climb the stairs to a newspaper

[119]

office where a certain editor sits at his desk eager for
colloquy. His stuff has all been put on the wire, but
he stays till two o'clock or so in case anything should
"break." He has comfortable chairs and he gets out
the bottle of Scotch. Then, if there are congenial
listeners, you may hear him unfold some of the richness
of his alert experience. Robert W. Service happened
to be in the other armchair the night I heard the story
of the cat. I don't identify the editor himself, for it is
his pride that in his twenty years on a famous paper his
name has only been printed twice, and then by accident.

He came down from Scotland as a youngster, to look
for a newspaper job. He tapped at all the doors and
found no entry. His small fund of money soon ran
out, and he felt himself beaten. There seemed no
room for him on Fleet Street, and one night he wrote
home asking for money enough to get back to Scotland.
He went to the post office to buy a stamp for the fatal
letter. On the counter sat a big black cat, comfortably
licking her fur. In an idle moment the young man held
out the stamp to see if the cat would moisten it for him.
She did so, seeming to relish the sweet taste of the gum.
He affixed the stamp and was about to drop the letter
down the slit——

Then he put the letter back in his pocket, ran to
a desk in the corner and then and there wrote a brief
story about the Stamp-Licking Cat at the Fleet Street
Post Office. How the postal authorities, always
solicitous of the public convenience, had laboriously
trained the animal to sit on the counter and lick
stamps for customers. How the cat was specially

nourished with a saliva-stimulating diet, and that a project was under way to mingle a little oil of catnip with the government's stamp-gum. And so on.

The first newspaper editor to whom he offered this agreeably preposterous little yarn accepted it with glee. It was the journalistic *coup* of the week. Illustrated papers wired for photos, and the Post Office was crowded with people asking to see the cat. The S. P. C. A. hurried round to see if it was a matter within their jurisdiction. The sale of stamps at that office increased forty per cent. And the author of the story has never since been without a job. It is the story of Dick Whittington over again, you see. I told you, didn't I, that England is all a kind of fairy tale. It is a different cat that my friend has now in his rooms in the Temple; but also perhaps one with magical powers. For when a Zeppelin dropped a bomb in the neighbouring quadrangle . . . it didn't explode.

The most unconscious pathos that I saw in London was a sign in an Oxford Street clothing shop. RAINCOATS FOR THE HOLIDAYS. (This, remember, was in summer.) And the most eloquent word was the name of the Air Ministry's building in Kingsway— ADASTRAL HOUSE. Which reminds me again of the journalist mentioned above. When the new Bush Building—a terrific loftiness by London standards—was put up at the foot of Kingsway, there was talk of building some living apartments on the roof, and renting them. Our Scot suggested an advertisement to lure possible tenants. "Yes," he said, quoting Stevenson— "Bed in the Bush with stars to see."

The Romany Stain

II

The American's first instinct is that a lively thunder-storm can't be far away. The spires of Wren point strangely pale among the dark jumble of the City, not unlike the white steeples of New England against a coming squall. That soft lilac light, diluted fuscous sunshine (it lies like honey in tranquil Bloomsbury squares) and shadows in a hundred blends and tints, surely they are some barometric omen. He almost pauses to listen, among the steady drum of traffic, for muted jars of thunder. But the air is light and fresh; fragrant, even in October, with almost April sweetness. In the bronzing squares it is a tender country whiff, though spiced always with that faint sharpness of London soot. London smoke, a gladness in the nostril, richest of all fumes to a cognoscenting nose. I recommend the great train-shed of Liverpool Street station at dusk as the perfect place to watch afternoon and evening plight their troth, with Smoke as the officiating spirit. Very sensibly did London choose scarlet as the colour for anything official—uniforms, post-office vans, pillar-boxes. One of our dark green letter boxes would be invisible across a London street. "Bring me my spear! O clouds, unfold! Bring me my Chariot of Fire!" cried William Blake. (We heard the organ at Canterbury Cathedral playing Parry's music for those stanzas the other afternoon—not among the "dark Satanic mills" but in the very heart of "England's green and pleasant land." It was good to hear Blake's great madman's voice exulting in the misty close.)

A Map of London

The Chariot of Fire, along a twilight street, is a post-office van.

A man who has only a few days in London would be very silly to spend much of his time writing about it. Better, for the moment, just to let the mind touch glancingly upon a few visions that seemed, somehow, of an essence. Getting off the channel-steamer at Dover, there was the engine *Sir Bors de Ganis* waiting to take the boat train to Victoria. Somehow a locomotive so named seemed adequate compensation for not having been able to see the chalk cliffs (the fog was too thick). And the train passed through Tonbridge, where I discerned two stations: one called Tonbridge Tub's Hill, the other Tonbridge Bat and Ball. It seemed a just entry into the land that invented sport.

Our first lunch was at Simpson's, off Cheapside, in the famous old Ordinary where the management tries to divert your mind from the amount of fish and eels you have eaten by offering a free meal if you guess the measurements of the cheese. England is surely the only country where fish is eaten three meals a day and again at supper after the theatre. Some enthusiasts even sally out at five o'clock to have a fried fish with their tea. A good deal of cockney wooing is done over platters of fish: the time, the plaice and the loved one all together. The statue of Britannia should wear a fillet of fish. Another gastronomy quite new to me was lower-case potatoes served in the soup. It was at a dinner where Sir James Barrie was at the board, and the host averred that Barrie had been brought up on potatoes in his soup. We all fell to heartily, hoping that the combination might have the same nimbling effect upon our own wits. Then, when the champagne was poured, a wag across the table begged for a potato in his glass. "I was brought up on it," he insisted. Perhaps (it just occurs to me) there is some meaning in the fact that the two greatest essayists England has had were named for food; and the third is half named for drink. All this took place in a room so lined with portraits by Hogarth that occasionally one lifted one's eyes from the table to remember that the painting of (was it?) the Woffington, "dallying and dangerous," was the one that Lamb had described.

The pearly haze that dreams over St. Paul's—the giant gooseberry as James Bone calls it, with the irreverence of a true lover, in his beautiful book "The London Perambulator" —is at least partly the steam of Sausages and Mashed rising from a thousand little taverns approached through narrow passages. There poets sit among barrels meditating their staves. At a few specially favoured places you can precede your sausage with a sublimation of Spain, which cork forests are grown to honour. The most teetotal of wives would hardly reproach her husband if he said he had lunched on Bristol Milk. It is the noblest of sherries. In the Fleet Street aroma there is also, when the breeze sets from Southwark, a rich gust of hops from the warehouses across the river. A blessing on the hop factors; it is their custom that has kept thriving unmarred one of the very last of the old coaching inns, the George in Southwark, only a few steps from the site of Harry Bailly's Tabard. There, in the words of an 18th-century bill still framed in the hostess's bar-parlour, customers will find "Beds, wines, spirits and stabling to their perfect satisfaction." The galleries of the inn overlook the yard just as they did when theatrical managers got their first notion from that sort of thing. The site of the Globe playhouse is near by, now built upon by the Barclay and Perkins brewery (a worthy successor; it was that brewery in whose affairs Doctor Johnson was, momentarily, an adviser; his head is still on their bottle-caps). And the Beargarden still runs down toward Bankside. The Three Hours for Lunch Club has established friendly relations with the George of Southwark; and that noble place has already its American reciprocities. Hopkinson Smith did a charming drawing of the coffee room and gave it to Miss Murray, the proprietress; it hangs there, watching the hop merchants playing dominoes after lunch; and on a table in the coffee room I found a much-thumbed copy of O. Henry's "Strictly Business." This was surely a surprise. I pointed it out to H. M. T., who was with us. "O. Henry just about saved some of our lives in the war," he said.

It is amusing to find a tiny Temperance Hotel bravely sandwiched in among the hop-warehouses. And the Club would be remiss if it didn't mention the Riverside Tea Rooms at 49 Bankside, which look cosily out over barges and cranes onto what must be almost the oldest and best view of London, with St. Paul's exactly opposite. It was pleasant to an American eye to find in low-lying Brixton, not far from Little Dorrit's church, the sign *Altitude, Ltd., Steeplejacks*. This was noted on the way to C. Morley and Co., wine merchants.

The Romany Stain

Mr. Morley was unfortunately absent, but his affairs were increased by four bottles of moderate port, purchased on the understanding that his first name, as I saw it last year in the telephone book, is Christopher. His assistant believes it to be Charles, but I am still hoping.

Since we've crossed the river to the beginning of the Canterbury trail we may as well go further. Canterbury, of course, is a Pilgrimage; and a pilgrimage is a journey made to some meaning that one feels is greater than one's self. There is a grave in the corner of a quiet, very fragrant ground in Canterbury, where yellow roses are still blooming in October. And there are two people to whom red carnations have a special meaning in London. One of these carnations, worn that day by chance, but crumpled after a long journey, was still in Titania's coat pocket. "Rest after toyle, port after stormy seas," we read on the stone; then, as we turned away, I saw her secretly take the flattened little sweetness from her pocket and put it among the many lovelier flowers on the grave.

James Bone, in that very remarkable book about London, the piety of twenty years' close watching and fine imagining, tells the story of a Cockney in Canada who enlisted for the War. In making out his paper he wrote simply *London* as his birthplace. "London?" said the recruiting officer. "Which London? London, Ontario?" "London, Ontario!" cried the outraged exile. "London, the whole bloody world!"

Yes, that's what it is. To the New Yorker its altitude seems limited; but like the potatoes in Barrie's soup, our hearts were brought up on it long before we were born.

L'HOMME QUI RIT

I HAD felt for a long time that it might happen; now it has. But first I must tell you how time and feeling led up to it. Life is always leading up to things; then—as in this case—you find yourself unprepared, and behave disgracefully.

It is the calm, suspended expectancy of autumn that has something to do with it. Over these coasts there now lingers the yellow quiet of October: as you bicycle softly through villages you smell cider on the air—the air that is so curiously mingled: it feels warm and smells cold; and sliding round a dropping bend you suddenly drift into a whole pool of moist chill. Red and yellow apples are piled in the fields; the eyes of donkeys are more wistful than ever; your wheels pass over little

[127]

prickly mats of flattened chestnut burs—just as they used to in the woods round Haverford, twenty-five years ago, before our chestnut trees all died. Perhaps good American chestnuts, when they die, go to France?

The season of *bains de mer* ended in mid-September, all the visitors are gone, the little town has settled down—after a disastrously wet season—to the long pull through the winter: you see the tradesmen apprehensively getting ready to live on one another. Old Julie, our tumultuous factotum, will shortly go back to her normal life as a fishwife. I wondered why she was so eager to have the Microcosm's baby carriage when we leave. Now the truth is out: she says it will be fine to sell fish in, *pour gagner ma petite vie pendant l'hiver*. But she must be careful to balance the fish in it just right, as we had to the baby, because it's one of those French prams that shut up suddenly into a kind of sandwich.

It's this drowsed and apprehensive sweetness of October that the *baïnsdemerists* miss by going back to Paris so early. Perhaps some day you'll go along the hidden leafy road from Donville to Mme. Lebrun-Hecquard's inn A la Rivière at Coudeville; where you can sit at a small yellow table under the passion flower—that strangely Freudian plant—and have whatever *consommation* you prefer. After your port wine (which the French drink *before* dinner, as a kind of cocktail, and very sensible, too), Madame having lit the fire in the little sitting room, you can tackle chicken *en cocotte* bathed in a noble gravy, and an omelet that has somehow inherited just a faint tingle of onion:

nothing so gross as the pearly bulb itself but the misted maiden tears of a young female onion in distress. It was there, with a bottle of *vin d'Anjou*, that we sat with a poet and his wife and after deploring the lack of reticence in the passion flower, fell upon a discussion of the private life of the Russian aristocracy. We knew a good deal about this, as one of us had employed a governess who had once worked for a Russian grandee: we concluded (about the time the *vin d'Anjou* was finished) that the Russian nobility had led the lives of passion flowers; but that the real reason for their goings-on was that they were a hot-climate race compelled to live in a cold country, and that this had made them mad.

It was when I went back to Madame Hecquard's, some time later, to retrieve my walking stick which I had left there that evening, also a notebook full of memoranda about some phantoms in a book that doesn't get written very fast, that I specially remarked this October vacancy and air of attendance. It is a sober landscape: no flame colours as at home, just a gentle subsidence into pale brown and saffron. But the violets are still in flower, and roses, and big cider casks, stoppered with a twist of straw, creak along the way. Or on these clear nights, on the grass-topped cliffs over the sea, the world is so still that one thinks one might almost arrive at some conclusion and yet turns uneasily away from that lucid sky because of its exquisite lack of meaning. A candy-peel slice of moon drifts down toward the rocks of Chausey, there is the heavy rattling crumble of high tide

on the stony strip of upper beach, a mild air with strong
grassy sweetness. How (one wonders) did we happen
upon this one stretch of uplifted lonely pasture, spread
superstitious above sea and bare to the night—just the
field that one's mind required? Some day—and as an
honorary member of the *Syndicat d'Initiative* of Don-
ville-les-Bains I suppose I should relish the idea—some
day people will build upon that field and even imagine they own it: but some of it will be mine, and I
and my phantoms will walk there unawares.

Now I am beginning to approach the matter. The
soft and ripened solemnities of autumn, the long
serenity of lonely sands, these tickled by the jovial
absurdities of bilingual ménage, all had long put me in
dangerous disequilibrium. That afternoon, it appears,
Julie had groaned more than usual. These groans—
which are not the expression of any undue torsion of
withers, but a combined whistle, sigh, grunt, pant, and
hallelujah, accompanied by a roaring sneeze and a
gargling of the glottis, are Julie's way of letting the
household know that she is on the job. For, if by
hazard as much as fifteen minutes have passed without
Julie's having an opportunity to talk to someone, she
begins to be doubtful of her own existence: she needs
reassurance.

I asked the Urchin—who finds Julie a phenomenon
as amazingly fascinating as a rainbow or a French
locomotive—what Julie was groaning so much about.
That's not groaning, he said, she's saying her prayers.
I said that I did not think those emanations were
exactly prayers, they seemed to me too vehement.

Oh, yes, they are her prayers, he insisted; she always says something about Jesus after each one.

—You don't know nearly all the funny things that go on in this house, he said presently.

—I'm glad I don't, I said sternly; I know quite enough; it's difficult not to laugh as it is.

—Julie, I said, you had better repose yourself a few moments and take a glass of wine.

—Monsieur, she replied, there isn't any more red wine. (I began to see why the specially rich wavelength of the groans.)

—Eh, well, Julie, take some of the white.

—Monsieur, the white wine takes me with strange drollery in the stomach.

A little later Julie returned to the matter of the small enamel coffee-pot which I bought for five francs and on which her heart is set.

—It is only six days from now, Monsieur, that you will call for your good little coffee and there will be no Julie to bring it all hot.

—Julie, I reply, you are managing my weaknesses; I implore you not to agitate me.

—You will think then, Monsieur, in America, of that poor maiden who will be under the earth for all you know, the poor maiden to whom you gave this jolly small coffee-pot as a souvenir.

—But, Julie, if I give you that coffee-pot (the old rascal has had a carriage load of things given her already) what shall I have as a souvenir of *you?*

More groans in the kitchen, later. This is because Julie knows that to-night we are going over the proprietor's inventory, and the fact that she has broken eight out of the ten coffee-cups will presently be discussed.

She begs us not to put the new ones, just bought for replacement, "in circulation" before we go. "I have," she truly says, "a very maladroit hand with cups."

But it was at the dinner table that it happened.

—Julie, these sardines are very good. I've left some for you.

—Monsieur, I adore them. But I can't take any: they lie at the bottom of my stomach for three days.

I could see them lying there; but I got by this corner safely. Then, forgetting she was not in the kitchen, Julie let off another groan. The tiny *salle à manger* vibrated.

—Julie, you groan much this evening.

—Sir, it is my unhappy feet. I have no blemish nowhere (she runs a patting hand over the superb rondures of her person) save in my feet. *Ils gonflent.*

It began to come. I couldn't help it. But she misunderstood my preliminary agitations.

Oui Monsieur, ils gonflent comme ça. And she seized the end of the bread-loaf to illustrate the size of those members when they *gonflent.*

It came. I laughed. I roared, I rocked, I cackled and wept and shook. The long restraint of months was broken, all Julie's adorable and maddening ways broke like surf on the pebbles of my mind, I caved in. I laughed . . . I laughed as a man laughs when he reads "L'Ile des Pingouins." How long is it since I have laughed like that?—Not since the *Saturday Review* was founded.

CURE OF SOULS

I. *SAXONIA*

I SAT down one evening, in the smokeroom of the
Saxonia, with a sandwich and a glass of toddy, to
write in my diary. How pleasant it would be (I
thought) to begin with the address 47° N, 36° W. But
steamship smokerooms aren't what they were in the
first chapter of "Captains Courageous." (Did you
ever wonder why the illustrator of that book drew a
picture of an Atlantic liner steaming through a Grand
Banks fog *with all her flags up?*) Just behind me a
lady was talking about Henry James. In another
corner a lady was winning a game of poker. On the
thwartship settee more ladies, in shimmering gowns
and long knee-crossed slopes of pale silk stocking, were

listening partly to a garrulous gentleman who said he was writing a book about God and partly to another who was narrating how in Dayton, Ohio, the inscrutable brightness of Pelmanism shone round about him and strengthened him to put over a big proposition upon a group of important customers. "A man will be what he wills to be," he concluded.

Born eavesdropper, I was not strong enough to occlude these agreeable distractions. Besides, I was merely jotting down, for my own pleasure, random attempts to define a work of art. "A work of art," I wrote, "is something composed in proportion; but which also reminds us of the uncomposable disproportion between the universe and the artist."—"A work of art" (I tried again) "is something which by the subtlety of its imperfection suggests the completeness we can never grasp." These absurdities, which gave me mild pleasure to consider, were probably the effect of reading Anatole France's delightful "Jardin d'Epicure"; for I am rational enough, in my proper senses, to know that a work of art needs no definition. If M. France had been in the smokeroom (I reflected) he would hardly have been idling over a solitary notebook and a hot Scotch. He would have been talking to the dark girl over there—the only one in the room whose voice was inaudible and stockings invisible. Or would he have been pondering the notice warning one against professional gamblers? How delightful an advertisement, I used to think: tantamount to warning us against the whole human race.

But the restless indolence of the sea was upon me:

even the bland, phosphorescent ironies of M. France were beginning to seem faintly sterile. I went to walk on deck: one of those long, vacant, hypnotic prowls that can only be taken, on shipboard, late at night. For during daytime there is a tacit agreement among passengers that no one must look at the sea. If you halt by the rail a moment to make friends with Space, someone is told off to Start a Conversation. Steamship companies, I believe, award promotion to their delightful pursers according to the number of social events—tennis tournaments, fancy-dress parties, dances, concerts—arranged to avert people's minds from that embarrassing reality, the Sea. The only time I actually saw a latitude crossing a longitude, in a star-shaped bubble of foam, I was called away to consider the problem of what ought to be done about taking up a collection for the orchestra. On the modern liner there is a deck for every amusement except thinking.

The beauty of the old *Saxonia* was that she isn't modern. How glad I was we had resisted a friend's temptation to come home in the *Berengaria*. The first moment we climbed into *Saxonia's* bowels, from the Cherbourg tender, wandering darkly through storerooms and holds and galleys and engine quarters until we reached the white cabin passages, I knew her for the honest old sweetheart she is, the kind of ship I used to cross in long ago, the kind of ship I understand. When I took my bath, next morning, I immediately resumed my boyhood habit of putting my head under water, to hear the engines more plainly. Perhaps not even McAndrew knew that trick for tallying the magnificent throb of those great cranks. And *Saxonia's* engines are worth listening to and worth seeing: no turbine oil-burning business, but the real hell-raising, crashing rhythm of quadruple-expansion cylinders, and an old-fashioned stokehold next door—not manned by Gene O'Neill's symbolical apes, but by calm and apparently cheerful fellows.

The night I speak of, I strolled aft and looked in through the brass-circled ports of the lounge, where dancing was going on. The Chief had tossed care aside for the moment and was in his dress uniform, sidling about with sailorly gusto and ingeniously steering his partners against the swing of the ship. This was a brave sign; the night before, when she was dipping her nose into great green hills, kicking her bronze fins into thin water astern, the Chief's brow was dark. After years in turbines this was his first voyage in the old *Saxonia* and there was much to ponder. While you and I were topside, hanging on to something, enjoying the scream of the gale (that had passed through the regulation stages of *moderate*, *fresh*, *strong*, into *full*) and that thrilling fall and quavering shudder of a ship lifting her screws into mere lather, the Chief was in dungarees paddling the bilges, watching the governor that automatically shuts down steam when she races, even crawling under boilers to see that they sat solid on their stools. For the Man Responsible takes few people's say-so in a new job. That was the kind of night when the upper deck of the big fast ships would have been unpleasant. But a solid old leisurely slows down to sixty-three revolutions, puts her snout creamily into it, and you don't even need the fiddles on the saloon tables.

Anything that is greatly loved, as an old ship is loved, deserves study and deserves open homage. There is a type of passenger who has been spoiled, by large cabins and running water and private baths, for the *Saxonia* sort of thing. But there are still some of us who like to know that we are aboard a ship, not a damned hotel; to whom the plain old companionways are a joy and every creak of see-saw corridors a deep music. As you lie in your narrow berth—"It's narrow, narrow make your bed and learn to lie your lane"— you study the honest pattern of bolts along the white girders overhead; you astonish to find how that cradling movement completes the whole meaning and sensation of life. So consoling, so lulling, such a perfection of curved restfulness, the creaking ease of a slow ship that takes her own time among big water seems to abolish the mind altogether. *"C'est un grand débarras,"* as M. France says.

The steamship companies, in their resolute desire to keep passengers amused, and in the immense complexity of their business, have somewhat forgotten the essentially metaphysical nature of sea voyage. But the tradition lingers in an unexpected place—the purser's Routine Book. I am proud of having been allowed to study this great document from end to end: it lists everything that has to be done and thought of by the ship's business manager, and you will not wonder that pursers have to wear little rainbows of ribbon on their bosoms to keep up their courage. But the important thing is that in the Routine Book passengers are always referred to as "souls."

So, abandoning the irrelevancy of mind, it is as a soul you travel—in the eleven-day ships, at any rate. And you become aware of a greater soul too, that of the ship herself. Gazing entranced at the roaring flicker of her stout pistons, or privileged a moment to visit the bridge (not the glassed-in conservatory of the newer craft, but the old naked dog-trot, open from wing to wing), or palavering with the Lord of Below, you begin to realize how very dear to seafaring men themselves is this old vessel that has nearly run her course. Take her how you will, in the very shape and feel of her there is an honourable loveliness that the grander sort almost miss by their sheer splendour. For the greatest ships of to-day are so marvellous that neither man nor ocean can quite live up to them: but in the *Saxonia* type both sides of the problem meet and unite in gracious content. That is why I do not hesitate to honour her by name, for ships need praise as women do. They tell me that after her quarter century she will be withdrawn: that the ship-breakers are covetous of her stout mahogany and brass. But I keep thinking of Bill the Electrical Greaser, who has lived with her dynamos ever since she first went out, more than twenty-four years ago. Bill, who would certainly lose his way if he went topside (I don't suppose he ever saw her from above) has lived with her, as men live with women and ships, for twenty-four years. And when they take her off, what will Bill do then?

Cure of Souls

II. *CARONIA*

There must be some secret merit in the pure vacancy of a pellucid voyage like this; though one who loves to see a ship putting her nose into it may confess a private disappointment. This is now the eighth day of warm transparent weather and ballroom sea. The first night there was fog, and the whistle hallooed steadily, that deep terrorizing groan rather like the voice of John Donne in a sermon. It is a fine romantic sound to hear —when nothing happens; though, after the Chief Officer's little afternoon lecture on boat-drill, you meditate, in your bunk (not yet knowing your stateroom by heart) the exact order in which you would move toward your wife's life-preserver, your trousers, and the little folder of American Express checks. But after that one vigil there was nothing to reef the merriment of our delightful skipper. His enchanting mirth was often heard; our only gales were those of laughter proceeding from the captain's table in the saloon. The laughter of sea-captains is a comforting sound in the ears of passengers. Long may Captain Hossack and his fine *Caronia* make such comely crossings. I suppose it is a weakness of mine to believe that every ship I travel in is loveliest of all; yet I don't see how any could be more gracious to my eye than this steady old lady. A perfect vessel, nobly planned. From the boot-hole to the brass expansion-plate (I wonder how many passengers noticed that, the thwartship suture that gives and takes when she pitches) I find her full of delights; and her cranks are just as impressive as my vanished *Saxonia's*.

The Romany Stain

There can be nothing against her except that she's faster than I knew: she turns off her 420 to 430 a day, even when three quarters of an hour have been lifted from the clock. I was a little disturbed by a sign saying that if any Rotarians on board would make themselves known, the Purser would try to arrange the weekly sacramental lunch; but the notice disappeared, so evidently there weren't any. I believe that *Caronia* must be almost the very last of the Older generation (she was built about 1905) for the smokeroom steward tried gallantly to obey orders and enforce the placard *The Smokeroom Is Reserved for Gentlemen:* but he soon gave up. What an agreeable smokeroom it is, too, with plain old panelling like a Georgian taproom and a real open fireplace—not a bed of cold glass nuggets with an electric light under 'em.

I knew a sea-captain who said he kept himself in good trim by walking round the boat-deck (in the old days it used to be called the "hurricane-deck," but there aren't hurricanes now as there were for wet little ships like the *Umbria* and *Etruria,* or the blessed old *Pennlands* and *Wæslands* and *Westernlands* and *Belgenlands* that sailed from Philadelphia in the windy nineties)—by walking round the boat-deck picking up, without bending his knees, the hairpins dropped by young women late at night. But even that calisthenic is impossible now that all the young women are shingled to the nape. It is the junior officer who gets the exercise, playing deck tennis with the clinker-built young women; it is my observation that the engineers play a more cunning game than the men from the bridge. I wonder why that is?

Cure of Souls

Except for such pleasing interims as meals, masquerade dances, deck tennis, or cards, the merely passenger mind retires into a hypnotized serenity. It is with gazing fed; it gapes patiently over the stainless gulf and finds it as full of possibility and yet as empty of reply as a vast blue ink-bottle. Here, on this warm broad teakwood rail, is the very attitude and home of meditation . . . but no meditations come. The only consideration that hovers in my mind, after a week of scrutiny, is that perhaps the universe itself does not think, but even implores others not to do so. With a curious kind of alarm I found myself recoiling from Keyserling's "Travel Diary of a Philosopher" which a generous publisher sent me for shipboard reading. It is exactly the kind of book I love, and on shore I shall devour it; but here, impossible. Just as I always need a few glasses of wine to unlimber my French, so the mind requires a few whiffs of the unease of earth to liberate its fatal and enjoyable reasonings. Here no literature but the merciful detective story, or the latest "Lunatic at Large" can enter in.

My nearest approach to literature has been Mr. A. Edward Newton's "The Greatest Book in the World," which I enjoyed as I enjoy all Mr. Newton's chattings; and when, to my great surprise, I found him saying "If I were sending a boy to college, I would choose Haverford," you may imagine that I believed Mr. Newton's book to be a worthy volume. I think that is only the second time, in the general literature of the world, that I have found that small and unpublicitied college mentioned. I was pleased. Speaking of Storer Clouston, a group of people were hot-Scotching in the smokeroom and more or less feeling their way into one another's tastes. Excellent progress was being made; there was a subtle suspicion that these were kinsprits. "Now," said one, "here is a very crucial question. Are you—I have a feeling that you are—Lunatic at Large kind of people?" Yes, a cunning question! For if they hadn't been they would merely have thought it an insult, and the matter would have ended. But with a scream of pleasure they cried "Indeed we are!" and all was well.

I think I must tell you of a great triumph, because it will never happen again. Smoking alone one evening I was accosted by a genial gentleman in the doll business. He told me a good deal about the increase in the American doll industry. "Did you know," I said, "that Great Britain has removed the tax on dolls' eyelashes?" This excited him enormously, as he had not known about it. Well, I had read it in the latest issue of the Manchester *Guardian*, which reached me the morning I sailed. Nothing, after that, could dissuade him from believing that I too was a disguised magnum in the doll traffic. The information was evidently important to him, and cheered him vastly.

I don't agree with the Caliph Newton in all his delightfully crotchety musings; I think him worse than unfair to Matthew Arnold, for instance; but then you come upon so magnificent a thing as this—on Dickens—

"Of nature, in the ordinary acceptance of that word, he knew nothing, cared nothing. London was to him a vast field in which wild flowers grew, the children of the poor, and he gathered them by armfuls."

When I found that I laid down the book with a tingle, climbed out of the steamer-chair, and went to the lonely northward deck to think it over. Has any one lately written a finer sentence?

Now, in an hour or so, we'll be sighting Land's End, and you know that prospective thrill after a week of space. No longer that slow and thoughtless feeling of mere existence, that one has in a clear calm midnight when the masthead is steady against the grainy sky. The Channel is opening her arms to us, the queer uneasiness returns, a whole Continent full of irregular verbs is waiting. And this morning when I went on deck I distinctly smelt England. For seven days we had the universe almost to ourselves. But even God, I think, was restless on the eighth day.

III. *TRANSYLVANIA*

Taking a bath at the Central Hotel, Glasgow, I had a feeling of being already at sea. For in a Glasgow bathroom you find yourself among the specially large and sturdy plumbing, deep enormous tubs and brass taps, so familiar to all travellers in the Clyde-built ships. To read the name of *Shanks and Co.*, *Barrhead*, written in a bathtub, has always been part of the flavour of sea-adventure; how often, simmering deep in hot slanting brine, I have hummed small private madrigals in honour of Messrs. Shanks.

It would take a number of pages justly to describe the various excitements of making one's first passage from Glasgow. The journey from Euston, eight happy hours in what must be one of the world's most comfortable trains, would be a theme by itself. It was odd that of all the named engines on the London Midland and Scottish line, I saw (in the yards at Crewe) the one that would give me the most surprise—an engine called *Charles Lamb*. The express that leaves Euston at 10 A. M. is timed (in October, anyhow) so that you get your glimpse of the Westmorland hills in the full shine of afternoon. Be sure to look out for the two pretty girls sitting on a stone bridge near Grayrigg; you pass them about 3:15. Then, after the very Long-Islandish country north of Carlisle, where just casually your eye catches little stations called Gretna and Lockerbie, you meet the first sunset shadows in the folds of Annandale. You'll not be wasting time drinking tea in the restaurant car; it's my guess you'll be standing in the corridor watching those lovely bare ridges, bronze as Roman helmets in honeyed light; sifted with opal in the rough ravines. And if you're a lover of differentials in language, the first thing you'll mark at the Central Station in Glasgow is the sign "*Passengers Are Requested to Shew Their Tickets.*"

Certainly philologists should always make the Glasgow passage; words that are strange and yet anciently familiar are like toys for you to play with all the way over. "Bute Hall," said one, showing me the Glasgow University by starlight. "Lord Bute?" I asked, "Aye, he gifted it." Going down to Greenock, where we boarded *Transylvania*, how pleasant to see the sign *Ground to Feu*. Speaking of calling us in the morning, "I'll just give you a chap on the door at 8 o'clock," said the steward. And the Chief Engineer, in one of those

midday cracks after the Captain has sent word from
the bridge that "the sun's over the foreyard," was telling of fishing for octopus. It's not bad meat if you
don't know what it is, was the gist of his comment;
"but if ye know, ye kind o' grue at it." There is some
lively etymology to be taken in at every turn. Walking
on the boat-deck, under the three black funnels, where
that fine soupy whiff comes up the galley ventilator and
sharpens the appetite, I found a small faucet marked
Boats' Breakers. Why, one might well ponder, is a life-
boat's water keg always called a *breaker*? The captain,
who could outskeat many a college Ph. D in his knowl-
edge of words, told me why. It's really *barreca*, Spanish
for a small cask. This pleased me, as I already knew
the French *barrique*. There is no lingo so savoury as
that of ships and charts. Even Cape Race, that ill-
favoured coast which masters give a generous offing in
foul weather, the Captain secretly relishes for being the
tip of the Avalon Peninsula. Of the names on the
Newfoundland chart I liked specially Random Sound:
it seems to carry the indignant voice of perplexed old
mariners. Pinchgut Tickle is another name I remember
on that chart. It was Joseph Conrad, in a little essay
not yet (I think) collected in his volumes, who praised
the kind of writing found in Notices to Mariners and
other sea-memoranda of that sort, where a lack of pre-
cision in the text may mean life or death.

We were not less lucky than John Burroughs in our
hap of weather. The Clyde, as he noted long ago in
"Fresh Fields," is the finest of all approaches to Britain;
when we went down the firth on a transparent October

afternoon it was at its best, reminding me of a grander Lake George. Glasgow has not been very skilful in letting the larger world know the magnificence of her noble waterway. We are all aware that she is a great shipbuilding city, but somehow we do not realize that she is approached by a winding strait among purple mountains that is surely among earth's finest picturesques. To an eye wonted to Long Island levels the fells and laws seem unexpectedly high and bluff. Goat Fell runs close upon 3000 feet; Ailsa Craig sheers up 1100 feet in one steep lump. As you glide so smoothly by the openings of a dozen lochs and sounds, each bending in among the unspoiled hills, or look over into the green apron of Ayrshire, it seems preposterous to leave this magic region barely glimpsed. I wonder if any other great manufacturing town has such fairylands at its door. By the time you have dropped the Mull of Kintyre, and Scotland fades, Rathlin Island (where the Bruce studied spiders) is in sight. It is too dark to see the Giants' Causeway, but even so to note near-by on the map such minstrel names as Coleraine and Limavady—yes, and Bushmills—gives a pensive pleasure. Off Moville the tender comes down from Derry with Irish emigrants to board the ship, a fiddler playing reels to keep their hearts up. It's a longish trip from Derry in the tender, and I imagine there may well be sore hearts among them; though some who come to see them off have much drink taken and are in very lyric mood. But the eldritch voice of the ship's whistle, as she gives the tender a final salute, seems almost a refinement of cruelty. It is so very definite. But it is part of the "drill," as our Scottish friends term any manner of rite; and at sea that is all-important. At Moville I received an Irish telegram, in a bright green envelope. The official notations on the form were all in Irish, beginning *Telegrafa an Phuist*, which somehow brightly conveys a suggestion of swift urgency.

Then, for a week, you are drowned in vacancy. What British weather-reports always call an "anti-cyclone" (not, as anxious females sometimes imagine, a specially violent kind of cyclone; but a period of prevailing high barometer) was with us; day after day of fresh breezy blue. A caller air, as one Scot called it. And you move in the slow and yet regularly measured circle of shipboard hours, aware of Time only in the same vague accepting way that one is aware of the surrounding sea. Almost with incredulity you read, a week later, that "Heavy baggage must be ready to be removed by 8 P. M." and they tell you that Nantucket Light Vessel will be "made" that afternoon. There were few passengers in the first cabin, and it seemed curiously like a house-party at some large country mansion. It would be true to say that the most exciting single event of the week (barring, of course, the little meetings when the Captain and the Chief talked unpublishably of the queer ways of the sea) was the night I had a vile cold. A kindly passenger gave me tablets of aspirin and phenacetin to take in the evening hot toddy. Later, as I lay gently tilting and steaming in my berth, I woke from marvellous dreams—dreams of half-apprehended glamour and magic; visions that drift away like smoke in moonlight but still leave behind them an uneasy suspicion of merriments and pangs beyond the humdrum of this daily plod. It was the kind of hypnotics most teasing of all: a dim continuation of something dreamed once before. I suppose that if it were not for the greatest peril of the sea (which is overeating) one might have more of these lovely clairvoyances on board ship. If only the steamship companies didn't feed one so well and so often, if one had the austerity to live for a week on toast and bovril and hot toddy, what golden fables might result.

And to-morrow morning we shall sight Liberty again. There's nothing so wholesome as to hear the little jokes people in other lands make about one's own country. A story now current on the other side is of a Frenchman making his first visit to America; and as he came up New York Bay an American pointed out the Statue of Liberty.

"Yes," said the Frenchman, "we do that too."

The American was puzzled. "Do what?"

"Put up statues to our dead."

THE FULL-GROWN POET

IT WAS perfectly delightful. I happened to be spending the afternoon with Q. U. when the literary editor came to interview him. I was a little troubled, because we had been talking rather unco matters, and the poet was in spate. He was in that characteristic vein where beauty and ribaldry are so strangely mixed: which must be kept dark at all costs so as not to disturb people. If he were to continue like that. . . .

"How do you do?" said the critic (at least that's how "Who's Who" lists him)—"Oh, hullo, Morley, you here? Well, well."

I made a motion to withdraw, but Q. shook his head. "Bill just wants to ask some insulting questions," he said. "I'd feel safer with a witness."

The Romany Stain

That's one of the things I love about Q., he always has the right thing to say (even in his poems).

Bill went straight to the point.

"You remember that thing of Whitman's," he said. "About the Full-Grown Poet. Well, never mind; what I mean is, I want to write a piece about you with that title; I feel that you are Full Grown, you've got stature; excuse my being so frank. One of the things I'd like to bring out in my piece is that people don't realize the extraordinary preliminary anguish of creation, how the damned thing is threaded out of your very bowels; the contemplations, postponements, futile gropings, horrors, that precede every work of art."

Q. replied by telling a bawdy story out of the book of Genesis, which was gruesomely apropos. I hoped Bill wouldn't allude to it in his article. Even in the Borzoi Classics (each copy numbered) a similar episode was omitted from the Confessions of old Jimjam Rousseau. But Bill's powers of omission are merely vestigial.

The interviewer swivelled his eyes a little wildly (I could see his quick retina netting a mental picture of Q.'s workroom to give local colour to his sketch). A taxi-driver, swerving a dangerous corner in thick traffic, sometimes shows just such a phobic glitter.

"Fine!" he exclaimed. "I see you agree with me. Now what I like about your stuff is that, in spite of these preliminary horrors, when it comes out it comes clean. Technically clean, I mean, of course. You know Gide, the great French critic—not nearly enough known over here—quotes some lines of Baudelaire

The Full-Grown Poet

which he says form the *motif* for a great treatise on
æsthetic. Order, beauty, luxury, calm, and voluptu-
ousness: that is Baudelaire's sequence; and Gide says
those are the elements of nourishment for any great
work of art. Oh, gosh, Gide is great stuff: whole
gangs of the young Frenchmen just stem right out of his
'Nourritures Terrestres.'"

"Out of his what?" inquired Q.

"His 'Terrestrial Nourishments,' one of his early
books, published in 1897. Think of it, he was only
twenty-eight when that book was written. It's a pity
our folks aren't wise to Gide."

"Surely he'd be a lot less useful to you if they were,"
Q. began mildly. . . .

"But just let me say this before I forget it," cried
Bill. "I forget whether it's Gide's idea, or my own
deduction from him, but the notion is (and I believe
you feel it too) that man is now *too* sharply sensitized,
too self-aware; Nature's great hankering for specific
self-consciousness has, in man's case, passed the
margin of decreasing returns (psychological returns, I
mean) and he's canted toward destruction. You know,
the Henry Adams dope."

Q.'s lips began that jolly curling pout that always
precedes one of his best, but Bill was leaning forward
with ardent face.

"There are some fellows getting up a scientific symposium on Sex," he continued. "Something really
detached, you know; genuine philosophical observation; there's always been too dam' much gross biology
in the Sex business; well, they've got a lot of really

unbiassed testimony in this thing, getting it down to harmonic rhythms, graphed in orgasmic curves; nothing prettier than those curves if you really get some perspective on them. Well, they've gotten frank comments from all sorts of authors and scientists, really liberal-minded people who understand the love life."

"Yes," said Q. firmly, "I've seen the thing. They sent it to me for my opinion. I showed it to—well, to a woman I know."

"Ah?" said Bill. I knew by his manner that he felt he had struck pay-dirt for his article. "What did she think of it?"

"She said, 'Those children had better get off the merry-go-round, they'll break their necks.'"

Bill grinned in his disarming way, but was not torpedoed. "Well, I don't know," he said. "These things are rather fundamental you know. For instance, they've discovered that organic life can actually be created by alternate light and darkness striking into shallow salt water. What is that but a corroboration of the old myth that 'Dame Venus, love's lady, was born of the sea'? Anyhow, it all comes back to Walt's doctrine: whatever tastes sweet to the most perfect person, that is finally right. Havelock Ellis approves that too. . . . But of course even the parson can quote Walt to his purpose. That's the beauty of Walt. He played everlastingly safe because he caromed off every cushion there is."

There was a moment of silence while Bill lit a cigarette. Q. creaked uneasily in his chair. His remarks are usually oblique to the course of the topic.

The Full-Grown Poet

"A terrible thing happened the other day," he said. "I had been reading a volume of very modern poems, some rather bully stuff too, but a bit eccentric in typography and so on. I happened to meet the author at a dinner, and complimented him heartily on his opening poem, which seemed to me a specially rich, frolicsome bit of incoherent outburst. To my distress he was obviously annoyed. When I got home I looked at the book again. What I had thought was his opening poem was really the table of contents. Really, it was quite fine."

"Another thing I want to bring out in my essay," said Bill, "is the dignity of your attitude. I don't mean your present posture, with your feet on the desk; but your attitude toward life, toward criticism. I like your bare and robust simplicity. So many poets are madly hastening about, busy lecturing and meeting fashionables, they positively don't have time to say what they think. Perhaps it's safer that way. But there's a sort of elemental massiveness about you, like Nature herself, who is strangely silent when interviewed but has her own secret convictions."

"That's just my trouble, Bill," said Q. "I haven't any convictions. But I feel sure that if we chin a while you'll find some for me. Better stay to dinner."

"I'm awfully sorry, old man, but I must catch that next train. Got my page to make up to-night." He began rummaging in his brief-case. I had a horrid fear that he was going to produce Q.'s new book and ask him to autograph it.

"Thanks awfully for letting me come," he said. "I

wanted to be sure I had the right slant on your ideas. If you want I can send you a proof, so you can be sure I quote you correctly. Here's a little thing I've brought you, my 'Ejaculations, First Series.' I've put your name in it for you."

He patted Q.'s shoulder affectionately, shook hands with me, invited us both to lunch, and started off. Then he turned back at the gate, his face shining with genial excitement.

"There's another line of Whitman's," he said, "that I'd like to quote you as saying. It's this: 'Let him who is without my poems be assassinated!'"

"Go to it," laughed Q. We watched the caller striding swiftly down the hill toward the station.

"Well," I said, "that's the kind of interviewer who makes it easy for you. I love his way of making you stand sponsor for his own ideas. Nice cheerful fellow, anyhow."

"Cheerful?" said Q. "Is that your idea of cheerful? Poor heroic devil."

A COFFEE–BAR

AS YOU go up the Boule' Mich', toward the Luxembourg Gardens, just above the famous old Café
de la Source (whose back door, opposite the Noctam-
bules cabaret, always suggests the beginning of a story)
you pass a little coffee-bar. Café-Bar de la Sorbonne
it calls itself; and I close my eyes for a moment to see it
plainly. Perhaps—indeed, very likely—it is a rainy
evening and you slip in there for a café-cognac to think
things over. At night it is a cave of various lights.
The line of little red bulbs under the pavement-
awning gives just a tender pink tinge to the air and to
the piles of numbered saucers. Farther in is that
magnificent terrace of bottles, some with green and blue
foils on their necks. The ceiling is some sort of violent
mosaic, the walls are mirrors, the cane chairs are striped
orange and black. The waiters are coasting swiftly

to and fro on the sliddery sawdusted floor, going from the bar to the larger room at the rear—*2 Billards Au Fond* says the sign—into which I never penetrated. The moist zinc counter sparkles with reflections of glassy, twinkling colours. Even the buttered tartines shine with a greasy, pinkish light. Behind the bar is the man in shirtsleeves, with prominent, friendly, much-enduring eyes. How often I used to meditate as to the exact shade of temperament suggested by those eyes, which I found as difficult to put a word to as even Conrad and Ford Madox Ford (the author with the reversible name) found their fields of dark blue cabbages. They were eyes naturally friendly, but also with an under-light of weariness, or alarm, or passive suspicion; or a knowing calmness toward the stratagems of men. Eyes which, by always expressing a tinge of faint surprise, seemed to guard against the likelihood of ever being surprised further. So at any rate I used to think while I was standing at the bar drinking my coffee. *Au Comptoir, Café 30 c*, says the sign. Another subject of pondering was whether the errand boy from the near-by shoe shop had the faintest idea what the gilt letters on his cap could mean. He wore a braided uniform and the inscription on his cap was a perpetual indignation to me. Here, in the bosom of the Quarter on an actual *gradus ad Parnassum*, what legend did I I find on that fellow's cap? PHITEESI, it said.

But it is not of the shoe-shop *chasseur* that I am really thinking. I am thinking of the girl, charmingly dressed in black, who used to come in every morning at the same time to ask if there was a letter. Perhaps people are more indiscreet in their letters in France, and find it advisable to have them sent to café-bars instead of to their homes? Are they afraid that the wrong person will read them? They needn't worry about *me*, bless them; I find even the most innocent French script hard enough to decipher when duly addressed to me. But, anyhow, quite a lot of people have their letters sent to that café-bar. (Perhaps that is why the shirt-sleeved proprietor shows that faint brightness of disillusion in his brown eyes.) And every morning the girl I speak of used to come in rapidly, go over to the corner of the bar where Shirtsleeves kept watch over his drawerful of small change, and ask if there was a letter. There was something delicately confidential in the way she asked: she did it more with her eyes than her voice. He would glance at the row of letters tucked into the foot of the mirror and gravely shake his head. Sometimes she was positive the letter was there, if he would only take it out from the row (politely arranged addresses inward so you couldn't spot the names). That third one from the left, it looked exactly (and I thought so, too) as though it were hers. But no.

She would console herself with a cup of black coffee, while I was sideways admiring the really charming trimness of her silhouette, seen against the bright flow of the Boulevard outside. It seemed to me detestable that she never got that letter. I even thought of writing one to her myself, if I had known exactly how to direct it. It would have been fun to watch her reading it. But, of course, it would only have troubled her. After her coffee she always flitted off rapidly, down the street, on her way to work, I suppose. I am still wondering whether she ever got the letter; and if so, I hope it said what she wanted to hear. Her chin, against the coffee-cup, was lovely. It was all I could see, under the *cloche* hat; but it was a very Parisian chin, showing a hint of resolute *jem'enfichisme*. So that even if the letter came, I feel sure the chin still has its small bravado.

Another woman in Paris. I had first seen her twelve years before, when she took my breath away: for I had always been told how much one ought to admire her. And I did, in a kind of dumb fool's amazement. So I went back to see her again.

You see her at the end of a long murmuring corridor. A long way off you see her whiteness: down that aisle that is full of moving people and the rustle of feet and hushed voices. She stands against dark curtains which seem black but prove, on approach, deep red. Tremulously, expecting the old thrill, you come near, disregarding the others who stand on each side the way. You have disregarded everything else—the huge Roman bathtubs (that would be so useful in some of the little Latin Quarter hotels) and the busts of Pallas. "That reminds me," said an American lady looking at one of these, "I want to go to Brentano's to see if the new *Ladies' Home Journal* has come in." And now you are in front of her—the Venus de Milo—and the old thrill doesn't vibrate.

The body—or as the American ladies say, the torso—is as noble as ever, but what has happened? It is heavy, muscular, sluggish. The face is void, drowsy, without meaning. How gladly you would sacrifice it to have the lost arms; which, perhaps, would bring her alive. You try to imagine what those great white arms could have been doing that would make her more a woman and less a goddess. Alas, she is just what a statue should never be—merely statuesque.

So I went away, wondering which one of us it was who had died in those twelve years. This, that we when young eagerly frequented, this that we were somehow taught to dream of as the ultimate perfection of classic form—well, how just that she seemed: how perfect and how formal and how stony. On any street corner I could see beauty that seemed more thrilling. But I was almost afraid to admit, even to myself, how disappointed I was. And then I was reading a recent issue of the *Transatlantic Review*. It is pleasant to admit that one always finds that magazine stimulating, because Mr. Ford Madox Ford (the editor with the reversible name) says: "A man whose culture is insufficient to let him read the *Transatlantic* with pleasure is practically no better than a savage." And in that journal I found Havelock Ellis admitting the same thing about the Venus of Melos. She had died on him as she had died on me. I loved her no less, of course; but what I loved was not her majestic, heavy grace, but the memory of my own youthful zeal.

To have my secret unhappiness confirmed by Mr. Ellis was a joy such as confirmation always is. I felt the same way when, the other day, walking on a Brooklyn street, Walter de la Mare suddenly burst

into praise of the mirthful magic of "The Wrong Box";
or when a Smith College girl asked me if there was in
the world another book as amusing as Hamish Miles's
"The Oxford Circus." For it is confirmation that
human beings most passionately seek. And if one
knew why all merely æsthetic opinions grow, flower,
and decay, one would know why it is that all the arts
move gently along their destined loops and returning
orbits. It would not be well to know, for we should
all be less instant in our small concerns. It is well to
feel sure of things while we may; and not remember
that even the Ten Commandments are only approxima-
tions. . . . Recurring Decimals.

BETWEEN TWO CHAPTERS

BETWEEN two chapters of a task that completely
absorbed him, a dream more real than any reality,
a workman paused, and came (as they say) to life.

Every day (he said to himself) is an artistic whole: it
comes out of nothing and goes back to nothing, like a
perfect story. Even if empty, futile, or absurd, it is an
orbed transaction. It is (you can't escape the phrase)
rounded by a sleep. What is that word they have for
people who are blundering somewhere too close to facts?
Yes, morbid.

Every day, could he control his impatience, offers
the workman the analogies he needs. Loneliness, self-
disgust, postponement, mirth. Though he added
"mirth" as an afterthought: for he suddenly realized
that there are days when you don't laugh. Of course,
one can always laugh on a moment's notice; but he was
thinking of the sudden whoops of unpremeditated cheer.

Such mirth as Pan and Cupid utter, sitting on a stump, when they think of the solemn rotarians on Olympus. These dejected them from the mountain-top because they were too mischievous for Heaven and kept spilling their ambrosia on the tablecloth. (Bibs had not been invented.) So, with no place in Heaven they had to suffer on earth as though they were men. They found it more fun: no wonder they laugh.

The workman saw it was difficult to keep his mind from going back to that crystalline abyss between the chapters. Yet he felt it wrong to go back at that moment: for the task was one in which reason, calculation, sense, could play little part. It had to be dreamed. Every man is sometimes interrupted in the course of his doings by a fit of brooding. But think of a task that is entirely brooding. He refreshed himself by adhering to that thought that every day offers the analogies one needs.

This workman had had, in one day, not less than six adventures. (1) A friendly parson had told him that another parson had told *him* "Every preacher should read 'Typhoon.'" This turned on a bulb in the workman's mind: a whole chain of coloured bulbs, as on a Christmas tree. (If one goes out they all go dark.) Yes, indeed: every preacher ought to read "Typhoon": he had never thought of it as a theological fable before. But it is, now, isn't it? (2) He was savage to a dog that had erred. This was a rambling dog of less than no reputation who had, at a critical passage of the workman's reverie, interrupted him by a gross misbehaviour —which was not, perhaps, its "fault." (Imagine talking of a dog's "fault." I can hear Pan cackling on his stump.) He chastised the poor brute, thrust it out into a very cold night. Soon he was troubled and went on the porch to whistle. But there was no answer. This set him reading Meredith: he remembered the poem about thrashing a dog. It is not a well-known poem, for Meredith marred it by stilted lingo. He thrashed the English language as well as the dog. He was not so good, maybe, at the simpler moralizings. His extraordinary jargon required subtler themes for its felicity. Take "Lord Ormont and His Aminta": magnificent passages, but how perilously close to Ouida is the general flavour.

(3) He saw a cat come up from the cellar and find unexpected scraps of fish in her plate. She flung herself upon them with a passion that revived his admiration of life. She crouched (her little propped elbows showing the lighter fur) purring and guzzling in ecstasy. He imagined how a tiger would look at a similar feast. (4) A child four years old, wearing only her shirt, was standing at a basin gravely washing her hands. He told her that a letter had come for her; that when she was ready for bed it would be read to her. She gave him brown eyes of solemn excitement. "And then I can have it?" she said. (5) He was chopping a dead tree, by a frozen pond. The sharp ax shore clean patterny slants into the pink wood. "She must have some of the noble flavour of wood-cutting," he said, thinking of someone in the task he was working on. "I've dipped her too far in darkness." (6) He woke from a dream. I will tell you the dream.

The Romany Stain

There was a tropical sand beach; and for some un-known reason it was imperative that he and another man should swim, at once, to the town that could be seen a mile or so away across the water. The town was on cliffs that were lilac against sunset; a lighthouse winked jewel-pale in the honey-coloured light. Others were on the beach, hastening them on. They had run down to look for a rowboat, which wasn't there. They must swim. There was no inkling as to the nature of the danger, but there was instant necessity. They waded into the water, which was shallow so that they had to wade a long way, the other man a little ahead. The sandy bottom was heavy and sticky, the water in that ruddy light seemed thick and viscid. It was full of strange weeds, ferns, clinging sponges of vegetation; there was a feeling of crabs. At last the water was deep enough for swimming, but as they threw them-selves forward for the struggle it seemed like liquid glue. They toiled and threshed in that warm slow element, like flies in molten amber; the level sun gilded them with mocking light, the distant cliffs deepened to violet, night was onward. The other man drew slowly, slowly ahead. It was impossible, it couldn't be done, it ended.

Among the thousand haunting analogies of every day, how is the workman to choose those which will minister to his job? Well, that is his affair. Reasoning can help little. He ensues that "selected proportioned il-lusion of life" of which Walter de la Mare spoke in his lecture on The Supernatural in Fiction. He cannot compete with life itself in its fecundity. Just as psychic or physical shocks happening to the gravid woman will have their effect on the unborn child, so is it with a writer in travail.

It is a hard doctrine (said the workman, as he timidly returned toward that strange emptiness lying between the ink and the vision) but it seems as though every day is the microcosm. Every day, from toothpaste to toothpaste, is an artistic whole; it offers the fables we need if we have the courage to scan them. There, at the edge of his crystalline abyss he stands waiting the uncalculable bridge of dream: and the work itself must be rounded by a sleep. What was it Anatole France said? "No book is worth writing if you can completely understand it."

A MIRROR FOR MAGISTRATES

THE Urchin and I were coming home from Balti-
more with a suitcase full of old books, good old
juvenile treasures such as "The Plant Hunters" (by
Captain Mayne Reid, I hope I don't have to tell you)
and "Voyage au Centre de la Terre" and "At the Back
of the North Wind"; and even the tattered family copy
of "Tom Holt's Log: A Tale of the Deep Sea." I
don't know who wrote it, for the binding and title-page
are both gone; and I don't know whether I dare reread
it, for it's sure to be a disappointment. But it con-
tains Polly, the first girl in fiction I ever fell in love with.

Of course, quite a nice piece could be written about
the sentimental pleasures of going along the shelves
of vanished boyhood and bringing back, with an eight-
year-old Urchin, some of the things that will now be his

excitement. But while he was deep in "The Boy's Own Indoor Book" (Lippincott, 1890), seduced by the same fascinating chapter on How to Make a Toy Locomotive that used to delight me, I was getting out some old schoolbooks from the suitcase. Here was the edition of Milton's "Minor" Poems that I had used—no, not so awfully long ago; in 1905, to be exact. I fell to reading the Notes, which fill 71 pages of small type. (The poems, only 56 pages of much larger.) Then, in the sweet retired solitude of the B. & O. smoker, Contemplation began to plume her feathers and let grow her wings.

I don't quite know how to admit you to the traffic of my somewhat painful meditatings except by quoting a few of the notes my startled eyes encountered. I had forgotten that schoolbooks are like that. It is astounding that any one ever grows up with a love for poetry. Was anything ever written more wholesomely to be enjoyed than "L'Allegro"? You remember the lines,

> *To hear the lark begin his flight,*
> *And, singing, startle the dull night,*
> *From his watch-tower in the skies,*
> *Till the dappled dawn doth rise;*
> *Then to come, in spite of sorrow,*
> *And at my window bid good-morrow* . . .

Fairly translucent, aren't they? Mark you then what the fifteen-year-old finds in the Notes:

Then to come, etc. This passage is obscure. (1)It may mean that the lark is to come to L'Allegro's

window and bid him "good-morrow." In this case
we must make *to come* and *bid* depend on *to hear* (41),
and suppose that the unusual *to* before *come* is made
necessary by the distance between it and the governing
verb. But such a construction is awkward. The interpretation, moreover, forces us to make the phrase
in spite of sorrow almost meaningless by applying it to
the lark; it makes it difficult to account for L'Allegro
seeing the performance of the cock described below
(51-52); and, finally, obliges us to suppose Milton ignor-
ant of the lark's habits, since the bird never approaches
human habitations—an ignorance we are not justified
in assuming if the passage can be explained in some
other way. (2) Another interpretation makes *to come*
and *bid* depend on *admit* (38). "Awakened by the
lark, the poet, after listening to that early song, arises
to give a blithe good-morrow at his window. Other
matin sounds are heard, and he goes forth," etc.
(Browne). Those who adopt this view explain that
he bids "good-morrow" to "the rising morn," "the
new day," or "the world in general." (3) Masson,
however, thinks that L'Allegro is already out of doors.
"Milton, or whoever the imaginary speaker is, asks
Mirth to admit him to her company and that of the
nymph Liberty, and to let him enjoy the pleasures natural to such companionship (38-40). He then goes on
to specify such pleasures, or to give examples of them.
The first (41-44) is that of the sensations of early morning, when, walking round a country cottage, one hears
the song of the mounting skylark, welcoming the signs
of sunrise. The second is that of coming to the cottage
window, looking in, and bidding a cheerful good-
morrow, through the sweet-brier, vine, or eglantine, to
those of the family who are also astir." This last interpretation is perhaps more in keeping with the good-
hearted sociability of L'Allegro's character. But see
Pattison, *Milton*, p. 23.

A Mirror for Magistrates

A little farther on we read in the poem that . . .

> *Every shepherd tells his tale*
> *Under the hawthorn in the dale.*

Tells his tale. Counts the number of his sheep (Warton, on the suggestion of Headley). For *tell* meaning "count" and *tale* meaning "number," see *Psalm* xlviii, 12, *Exodus* v, 8, though it must be confessed that when *tell* and *tale* are combined, as in the present passage, "the almost invariable meaning is to narrate something" (Keightley). In view of this last fact, *tells his tale* is also interpreted as "relates his story"—*tale* being taken either in the general sense of "any story" or in the particular sense of "a love-tale." "But (1) this [particular sense] would be a somewhat abrupt use of the word *tale*. (2) The *every* shows that some piece of business is meant. (3) The context too shows that. (4) The early dawn is scarcely the time for love-making."

Signor Allegro mentions mountains. The Notes retort smartly "There are no mountains in the vicinity of Horton, where Milton probably wrote these poems." The poem refers to "towers and battlements"; Notes give us: "These," says Masson, "are almost evidently Windsor Castle." "With wanton heed and giddy cunning," writes Milton, having a gorgeous time (his pen spinning merrily for the instant) but Notes pluck us back with "The figure is an oxymoron; consult a dictionary and explain."

Truly, like the drudging goblin, the editor's

> . . . *shadowy flail hath threshed the corn*
> *That ten day-laborers could not end.*

The Romany Stain

Fortunately our friend Morning Face, at fifteen, pays little attention to the insinuating questions and cross-references of the editor. Nor do I wish to seem unkind. This sort of small-beer parsing has, I dare say, its usefulness. In the voice of genuine magistrates it may even be thrilling. But heavens! Do you intend children to read poetry as though it were a railway time-table?

In lines 317–18 of "Comus" Milton speaks (very prettily) of the "low-roosted lark" rousing from "her thatched pallet." I spare you the scholastic editor's explanation that "low-roosted lark" means "the lark in her low resting-place," and that "roost, even to-day, is used figuratively for any temporary resting-place." But on "thatched pallet" he is beyond price. Oyez:

> *Thatched*, as Masson suggests, may here refer to the texture of the nest itself, and not to the covering. Keightley, however, says: "The ideas here belong rather to a henhouse than to the resting-place of the lark, which has no *thatch* over it, and in which, as it is on the ground, he does not *roost.*

I'm sorry: I can't go on quoting these nonsenses. If the pupil paid any genuine attention to them, which probably he doesn't, he'd get a queer kind of notion of how Milton wrote. He'd imagine that "Comus" was put together with the author's eyes on Homer, Virgil, Ovid, Horace, Shakespeare, and what not, picking out the plums. Of course, a thing like "Comus" is likely to pass like a swoon over the head of Fifteen anyhow; it is too full of the things that no gross ear can hear. Yet it would seem that an annotator might say less about the Earl of Bridgewater and more of the fact that the masque was written by a boy of twenty-five, which accounts for so much that is gloriously Bachelor-of-Artish in it. Instead of memoranda about "pleonasms" and "quadrisyllables" it would perhaps make the thing more human to the luckless pupil if he realized that the Lady was so obviously a phantom of a high-minded young celibate's imagination. How delightfully young-Miltonian she is: how differently he would have done her after his marriage to Miss Powell. And the simpering and gooseberry-headed Brothers. . . . But I'm not a teacher of literature, I have no right, probably, to expose my own ideas about such matters. After reading through the Notes on "Comus" in this very reputable edition (still used by thousands of children) I seemed to have been present at a murder. I could see the corpse of Milton in the ditch, and the bloody Piemontese—or was it the Modern Language Association—marching in lock-step down the highway.

The disturbing part of it all is that it renews the unpleasant suspicion that the professional teachers of "English" do not always have any very clear idea of what literature is all about, or how it is created. Such pitiable haggling over absurd irrelevancies is, in Don Marquis's fine phrase, to play veterinary to the horse with wings. Poetry, God help us, is men's own hearts and lives; it is both a confession and a concealment. It rarely means exactly what it seems to. If we knew why Milton reached his most magnificent vibrations of eloquence when speaking for Comus and for Satan we might know why—in the good old Lexicographer's phrase—he suffered at Cambridge "the publick indignity of corporal correction."

Poetry happens when a mind bursts into a sudden blaze; and the annotators gather round, warming their hands at a discreet distance as they remark that such and such a glowing ember is an echo from Horace or Virgil, or a description of Windsor Castle. As though a poet like Milton, in his godlike fit, gives a damn where the mysterious suggestion arose. To margent loveliness with such trivial scribble is (let's adapt one of Comus's own lines) to live like Poetry's bastards, not her sons. How shall we justify the ways— not of God to man, but of teachers to literature? And you will hunt in vain in the textbooks for the most human tribute ever paid to Milton. It is this: the only time Wordsworth ever got drunk was when he visited Milton's old rooms at Cambridge.

A PACKAGE

THERE is a passage at the end of "Alice in Wonderland" that excellently describes how some farmyard sounds, recurring under the dream, gradually break through the mist of Alice's fancy and bring her two worlds into one.

Living in a dream at Donville in Normandy, there were three special sounds, endlessly repeated, that used to come chiming through the uneasy apprehensions of one who sat in a thatched cottage trying to write. The jingling bells of the baker's high-wheeled cart and other *fournisseurs* who sped merrily outside our stone wall. The sudden appalling outcry of donkeys, like the scream of a rusty pump-handle. And, behind all other voices, the solemn hoot of the narrow-gauge train on the

Chemin de Fer de la Manche. Such a little railway, and it took itself with such charming seriousness.

Yes, I am thinking this morning of those serious little trains that go trundling northward from Granville, through Bréhal with its slender spire, and Chanteloup with its château, along the green trough of the Sienne; past Gavray and Hambye (where is the ruined abbey) to Percy and Tessy. I can see the little engine, with two jacks on the bumper ready to hoist it back on the track if anything goes wrong. The engine has very tiny drive-wheels and a very tall smokestack; on the front of the boiler is a big handle that makes it look more than ever like a toy to be wound up. Then there come a couple of freight cars, and two wagons for passengers. There is a first-class compartment upholstered in red leather, but I never saw any one riding in it. Along the top of each car is a signboard that recommends *Benedictine* or *Amer Picon* or something else to drink. And you sit on the wooden seats and watch the butterflies scared up in clouds as you go puffing through the slanting Norman meadows at perhaps ten miles an hour. At Bréhal you wait fifteen or twenty minutes while they shunt on a truck of baled seaweed. At Ver (the right name for a fishing village) the anglers get in with their creels of catch.

I like the Chemin de Fer de la Manche for taking itself seriously. Even when it misses the connection at Cérences (where it crosses the full-sized railway) you won't get any humility out of the young conductor. With a horn to squawk, a whistle to blow, a big leather box full of tickets of different colours and rat-

A Package

ings, all sorts of miscellaneous baggages to hoist on and off, and a big turnip watch to look at now and then, he is a felicitous youth. I only wish he were a little more powerful, considering the weight of some of the dunnage he hefts. I have a horrid feeling that he is overstraining himself sometimes.

But now you are wondering why I am thinking of the Chemin de Fer de la Manche this morning, and why I can suddenly hear the dignified and continuous whistle of that little train. (It would go faster, I think, if the proud engineer didn't spend so much steam in whistling.) I will tell you why.

One of the pleasant perplexities in going abroad and then coming home again is connected with the matter of parcels. In spite of careful instructions, people will mail packages to your foreign address. They arrive after you have left, and then what happens?

There are several stations of the C. F. M. in Donville: in this way Donville and the railway, though both very small, keep up their self-esteem. There is Donville-Blancs Arbres, for instance, and Donville-Something Else, and Donville-Triage. (Just what *Triage* means I never could quite find out.) These stations are all very minute, but they are carefully listed on the time-table. Donville-Triage was *our* station. And the other day I get a letter from the station-master at Donville-Triage. I am sure he remembers me; he will not have forgotten how, the first time I wanted to take a ride on the C. F. M., I went down to call on him the evening before to present my compliments, apprise him of my intentions, and get all the dope. I wanted to know specially how to buy the right kind of ticket for riding in one of those open carriages. I must effectuate my traject in full air was what I told him. He was pleased at my enthusiasm and promised me everything. But then when the train came (it leaves Donville-Triage at 10:15, in case you should want to take it) they had left off the open carriages that day.

Well, it appears from the Chef de Gare's letter that someone, whose name he puts down as Fibert Saint Phila (my guess is that it's someone on Filbert Street, Philadelphia, but I have no notion who) has sent me a package, and the question is what shall be done about it. I believe, for the honour of the Chemin de Fer de la Manche, I will copy the letter in exact translation:

Station of DONVILLE-TRIAGE
27 December, 1924.

Dear Sir:
There is arrived in the Station addressed to you, dispatched by Mr. Fibert Saint Phila, merchandises as follows:

1 Postal Packet

which are at your disposition against the sum of
O Fr. 86 for carriage
O Fr. 25 for expense of notification
Total 1 Fr. 11.

I pray you to have these merchandises carried away immediately, warning you that at the expiration of the hereinunder-indicated delay they will be submitted to the legalities of storage determined by the tariff.

The person who will take delivery in the Station will have to be bearer of the present letter fortified by your signature at the bottom of the following notice.

If they were not lifted away from the Station in the

[176]

A Package

48 hours from the putting to post of the present letter of advice, they would be able to be trucked away from the office, and without other warning, into a public magazine, where they would remain at your disposition.

I have the honour to salute you.

THE CHIEF OF THE STATION.

My first thought on receiving this was to write to the friendly Chef de Gare saying that whatever may be in the parcel I will give it him as a present. But, with my usual slackness about letters, I didn't do so; besides, that might involve all sorts of legal correspondence, signing of international waivers and what not. I remember what trouble I got into when a friend of mine, touched by my wails about French pipe-fuel, sent me a package of tobacco from America. I was pursued all summer by mandamuses from Paris urging me to appear and explain why I was importing contraband. I think the best thing to do is allow the Donville-Triage station-master to believe me dead.

Besides, the parcel is probably only a book to autograph. Few people realize how much woe has been caused in this world by the two Eddies (Eddie Bok and Eddie Newton) who wrote books describing how they began when very young to collect autographs and never took No for an answer. There isn't a mail nowadays arriving in the home of any one who ever published a book that doesn't contain letters from Young Collectors. They even send you the wretched books, taking it for granted you'll sign them and wrap them up and send them back. And then, by-and-bye, they write and accuse you of theft.

But I like to think that the little train came puffing up the valley from Granville to Donville-Triage, along the Road of Iron of the Sleeve, carrying a package with my name on it.

The Chief of Station, looking over his records, must occasionally see that name and wonder what became of the strangely eloquent and ungrammatical alien. He will not realize, perhaps, that I wear a part of my heart in La Manche.

A BIRTHDAY LETTER

(*February 10, 1925*)

YOU understood about human weakness, so you
will know how it is that I have left writing for
your birthday until this last possible moment. I've
been looking over some of your old letters. I don't
do so often, it is too troublesome to see how some have
misfeatured you. Then last night, about bread-and-
cheese time—the *wishing* time of the evening you used
to call it, when one rather hankers for some friend to
drop in (to get between one's self and Eternity)—I
began gaping stupidly into the fire, wondering how to
light a candle for your cake. It was a different fire
from yours: a fire of logs: wood that might have been
made into desks. It was silly of me to sit brooding

there, for to you of all men a letter should be the un-
studied excess of the mind. But it was the distance
between us, as snow was sifting, that chilled my fingers.
You have said pleasant things about the difficulties of
Distant Correspondence; but no letter was ever addressed you from so far as this. I sat there, empty of
everything but angry love. I could not write, so in
your honour I had some hot water with its Better
Adjunct, and went to bed.

What can I tell you that would interest you most?
There are still Richardsons about (you remember him,
the fellow who used to keep you waiting for your holidays? What an uneasy immortality he got himself
thereby); and fellows like Rickman, of whom you said
that he didn't have to be told a thing twice, are still
rare birds. But it is as impossible to be bored on
Murray Hill as it was on Fleet Street. Your old
anxieties about abstaining from tobacco and liquor
would be made more metaphysical here, since the
abstention is supposed to be compulsory. You'd be
amused, if you knew how you are regarded as a gospel
for the young, "studied" in schools, your desperate
and special humour conned as a textbook of "whimsi-
cality." Yes, they still label you "the gentle." They
have forgotten your letters to S. T. C., imploring him
to substitute drunken, shabby, unshaven, cross-eyed,
stammering, or any other epithet that rang true in your
ear. So endlessly has your "gentleness" been drum-
med into young ears that there has been, among our
more savage juniors, a kind of odd blindness as to the
real you. Perhaps they do not know you as you are

A Birthday Letter

in your letters. The rest of you, I must confess, it is long since I read. I am not a systematic reader, I love to gather my notions of people from their casual ejaculations rather than where they open themselves deliberately. So it is in your letters that I have you and hold you. There you have taught us, more than a hundred novelists could do, what love means. It suffers long and is kind. There I see your trouble and weakness so much greater than many others' strength. There I see you laughing at solemn apes; I see your divine silliness and your rich shrewdness. Sometimes, when my self-pitying generation beats its breast, I think of your magnanimous patience. I think of your rockets of absurdity, sent up like sea signals on a dark sky of loneliness. I think of those last days when you and Mary said that the auction posters were your playbills. I think of your great love story—yours and Mary's—perhaps the bravest in the world. Then I wonder whether some of us nowadays should not write an *Apologia pro Vita Sua*—an Apology for living in a Sewer.

You could remember "few specialties in your life," you wrote once for someone (a publisher, perhaps?) who wanted a blurb about you. Except, you added, that you "once caught a swallow flying." Indeed you did: the wild fierce bird of laughter with wet eyes. I think that to have known you when you had been walking arm in arm with Barleycorn and cast no shadow on the pavements of Covent Garden would have been very close to my idea of religion. I smile, as you did, to remember that the Woodbridge Book Club blackballed your volume. There was something in it—they did not know just what—that was not quite seemly. This implicates me, too, for some of my forbears, I suspect, may have cast a black pellet or so in that matter. I apologize: and neither of us loves them any the less for their genteel simplicity. And indeed that strange fancy of yours, when brightened into flame by understanding intercourse, must have been a lovely and reproachable sight.

We shall receive no letters in the grave, someone said: Doctor Johnson, perhaps. It is just as well, for you would scarcely relish this one. But it had to be written. If there are 150 candles on this cake of yours, they will be put there by the 150 who think of you not as the gentle, but as the tormented, desperate, mad, and tipsy Elia. Still, as you said of the "Ancient Mariner," literature can sting us through sufferings into high pleasure. "I shall never like tripe again." Once you wrote "I never saw a hero; I wonder how they look." Ah, dear Charles, you need not have searched far. Mary could have told you.

THE MATERIAL TO THE ARTIST

I HAVE seen it coming on. Now it must be said. It is my dangerous privilege to tell you what I seem to have discerned.

Happiest, unhappiest of creatures! Do you know what you are? I will tell you. I will tell you, though I hate the word, misused by thousands of canting weathercocks. Yet among those who have taken out their passports for that foreign land the word is still valid. Poor soul, you are an artist.

You are an artist; an artist in the true sense; in the sense that thousands of men and women who never set hand to manuscript or canvas or clay, who work in offices and ride in daily elevators and tend babies in the suburbs, are also artists. You are an artist because you feel; yet mere feeling does not make you an artist. You are not an artist because you are unhappy, or because you are wilful, or because you are impatient with conventions and things that rhyme with long ago. No,

my dear; the artist, more than any other, values conventions at their high serene worth. Conventions—
comings together—of the apt congruent mood, circumstance, intuition. And when he ruptures convention he does it consciously, meaningly, that the
audience may be aware the convention exists. "I can
do without God," one may have said to himself. But
the mere so saying proves His existence. You are an
artist because you feel—and control and modulate
your feelings. "Waking life is a dream controlled,"
said Santayana.

You are an artist, my dear, because you are aware
of the rich medium of pathos, absurdity, glamour, in
which all human actions are set. You are an artist
because you are aware. Aware of those little characteristic things, those strange revealing episodes, out-
croppings of mirth, of horror, that typify the whole of
life in miniature. You are a microscope. You are
an artist in the sense that the cubist painter Nevinson
is an artist, the poet de la Mare is an artist, the architect Gilbert is an artist, the paragrapher Adams is an
artist. You see the world in a grain of sand. It is no
credit to you. That queer besetting sense of values
was born in you, somehow. A wind blew—a mandrake
root yelped—a star slid—there it was. You found in
your heart that mad conviction that the whole gigantic
show of earth and behaviour was set in motion for you
alone. That the planet has laboured and created
railway terminals and terraced buildings and beautiful
women and toy balloons and subway cars full of dogged
faces—for you, for your devoted amazement. For

you, for this your moment of pitiful scrutiny, for this latest tremor of crumbling Now, the vast edifice of fairy tale swinked upward. Like the fiery bird of fable, you rise from red embers of poor burning selves and ecstasies forlorn. In this glory of you, you can afford to be humble. Lord help you, happiest, unhappiest of creatures.

And what have I to do with this? I am acting merely, for the instant, as the material for your art (don't misunderstand me). I am spokesman for the empty paper, proxy for the chunk of stone. I know that you will blunder; that you will see falsely; overboldly perhaps, overtimidly perhaps. I know you will be troubled. "A tadpole in a sea of flame," someone said. But your hunger will carry you through—your hunger for human contact, your passion for honest human value. This power, this power that is in you, will blunder; will warm you with shame in your lonely bed at night. But, knowing how your thoughts run, of one thing I am certain. You will never overdraw your account in the greatest security of all. You love life, and none of your checks on that commodity will come back cancelled *No Funds*. Let me give you, for your private ledger, three mottoes. Here they are:

It is only the generous who give to the rich, the big who praise the big; the niggardly salve their consciences in doles to the humbly poor, making life into a pilgrimage of greedy patrons in search of grateful victims.

ELIZABETH BIBESCO.

The nobler a soul is, the more objects of compassion it hath. BACON.

[185]

The Romany Stain

I wear a high hat because it's a charm against passion.
—From "Roger Bloomer," by J. H. Lawson.

This last—how superb it is—from that remarkable play by John Howard Lawson is, though ironically uttered, the perfect sentiment for the artist. He must have passion; but he must charm it; he must sing to it; he must soothe it to his needs, to the needs of other desperadoes.

Does that sound cowardly? Is it praise of the small sconced glim rather than of the blazing torch and cresset—that lights fools and wise men both the way to dusty death? I don't know; nor any man. Nor does it matter. The wind of your desire will move through you and speed you in your own channels. You will hardly even know how you have chosen. Being what you are, I know—aye, too well I know—that I (only a mouthpiece here in behalf of your still blank foolscap) can teach you nothing of the meaning of the artist's desire. Yet (I speak as the voice of your unwritten dreams) the anxiety of the Material is no less real than the yearning of the Workman. I shall blow through you as the wind; pattern your darkness as the stars. And even that will not be enough. Oh, brave fabric of life, that waits to be possessed, moulded, held and shaped and kenned. You have had the heroics so far; now let me speak the lines. Can the Pen (which is you) tell the Paper (which am I) anything about wanting? Poems must be lived before they can be written, I heard you say. Aye, but who has more fully lived the wistful poem of not being fulfilled? It is I,

The Material to the Artist

not you, that shall be the mover. I shall wet your nib and I shall speed your hand. Passion, pride and fury, and pitiable humility, too—these are mine. Are they less noble than your small zeal of achievement? I shall be God; you the ritual. You shall never possess me. "Grave is her shape, and sweeter unpossessed." Yet . . . it was not she who said so.

To some such purpose, maybe, the fabric speaks to the fabricator. And now, returning to our original parts—beloved and lucky rascal, I repeat it: you are an artist. You are an artist because you see the shadows cast by the actors. Life, clumsy or malicious electrician, throws crosswise shafts upon his puppets; each is mimicked not only by one shadow but by several. You are aware of these shadows, which so many do not see. Are you a *creative* artist? Is your trouble such that it forces you to communicate it? That I cannot tell. In any case, these strange, self-comforting, and self-harassing perceptions of ours must be our best consolation. They must be the shadow of the great rock in a weary land. Even so, a shadow is never more than a shadow.

My mind goes back again to that play, "Roger Bloomer," which I have just read. A strange little play; very young in its rebellions; very old (as old as "Faust," whatever the childlike critics may say) in its jolly and ingenious technique. There are some closing lines that struck me as nobly fine:

I've given you yourself, take it. . . . Face the music, falling about you like rain.

[187]

JAMIE COMES TO HY-BRASIL

GREAT things happen: sometimes in a burst of instantaneous completion; oftenertimes by slow indignations, through every grade of postponement, doubtful addition, and nail-paring disgust. But they do happen, and sooner or later the man with a blessing hears about them. The magic that moves our days brings us, by unsuspected curvature, home to ourselves. Believing our path to be a straight line—and going up, of course—we do not feel it leaning and bending beneath us, nor know it was a circle until we hear ourselves repeating what we said before—in a little louder voice.

The beginning of this particular magic (so far as I am blessed by it) was one snowy day when an enchanter (you would not have known him as such, if you saw him carrying a black leather suitcase and bulged about with a greatcoat from which I saw a glass phial protruding) descended from the train at Manhasset. Certainly it would take too long to tell you about this enchanter, how we sat by the fire together, how it snowed, how he went to a meeting of the Poetry Society that night (against all my advice, for nothing so surely nips the deep root of poetry in the breast as annual dinners of Poetry Societies), and what he wrote to me about it afterward. I will merely call this enchanter Tom, since that is his name.

While we were sitting at lunch Tom was narrating a passage from a book he had read. It was an Irish book and Tom being Irish himself he conveyed the full flavour of it. It was one of the most thrilling feats of memory that I have ever applauded: it was not memory but re-creation. He recounted, in the just accent, the tale of three notable miscreants who were hanged. One of these malefactors was annoyed because there were not enough women present. Another was bored, and yawned so gappingly that the executioner could hardly adjust the rope, and reproached him for his rudeness. The third was so thirsty that even as he swung he could not die until he had been taken down and given a drink. I give you these bald details merely because, so given, they sound nothing at all. But when you read them—or hear them in the Irish voice—they become that small bonfire of mirth, gilding the lower branches of the dark Tree of Life, that we call literature. Even the children at the table forgot to prattle while Tom told this story.

The Romany Stain

The book it comes from, though by one of the authors who means most to me, I had not encountered. I had not even heard of it. Then, a few days later, I saw it in a bookstore. I averted my eyes, for I was accompanied by several under-nourished phantoms of my own who were clamouring for blood, and I did not want to hearten myself with other men's ghosts. But then, not half an hour afterward, in the cabinet of another enchanter, whom we will call Mitchell (also, by odd coincidence, his name), I saw the book again. I opened it and began to read; I saw, what I had not been quite certain of, that it was the same that Tom had mentioned. "Take it along," said Mitchell. I was so eager to do so that I tried to persuade him not to give it to me. "Nonsense," he said, "I have two copies. I always buy two copies of every book, so I can give one away."

And then, the third enchantment. I was going home in the train, two or three days later. I was approaching the end of the book; approaching it with dismay, as one struggles to wrap round him the dissolving shreds of a dream that is about to vanish. The man in the seat beside me must have been a third magician, though I had not guessed it, for he was reading the *Evening Journal* and wore a particularly Hollywood shape of hat. He got out at Great Neck and left his paper on the seat. I laid down my book with the notion that Mr. Hearst would surely have provided something sufficiently grotesque to ease me of the exquisite pang of what I had been reading. And the very first thing I see in the *Journal* is an appalling photo-

[190]

graph of the author of my precious book; and an interview with him; he had landed in New York that day.

This does not prove anything. (What does?) But it suggests that it is not well to neglect the magic that moves round us. If you sew together enough random scraps of it you will have an apron of fig-leaves almost large enough to conceal you from the world. And it set me thinking as to how the man who wrote that book might better have been welcomed to New York than by the interview in the *Journal*, which purported in a noisy way to elicit his views on Love; or even than the photograph, which showed him in a hat quite as distressful as the one that got off at Great Neck, or the plush horror that I am wearing myself at this moment because I am going to the theatre this evening. How, I wondered, should James Stephens have been met; and what could be said? For that is his name; the James Stephens who wrote "The Demi-Gods," and who wrote the book of which I speak here—"In the Land of Youth."

This is a question to which there can be no answer. Literary criticism is a fine and fecund art; as some writers perform it—for example, William Gerhardi, in his book on Chehov, which does not seem to have received its due honour—it is an excitement and a warmth in the mind that linger for months after the reading. But a book such as "In the Land of Youth" transcends the realm in which criticism is viable. It is unmixed moonlight; moonlight neat. It fulfils that beautiful truth that Mr. Gerhardi (in the Chehov book) laid down—"A work of art whose aim and meaning were quite clear to the writer in the act of writing it would perish, as the universe would perish if its aim was clearly known to it." In the case of such a book, people who can enjoy it will need no help; and those who cannot could never be taught how. For the author of such a book the only just reception (perhaps) would be to have no one meet him at all: to have the pier and the dockside streets cleared of any one who might possibly know who he was; and to have every publisher in town herded in the lobby of some hotel until, at the touch of a hand-bell, Mr. Stephens appeared, with a gay symbolic gesture, to release them. I am not joking: for it is such men as Mr. Stephens who justify the existence of publishers and make their lives interesting and their jovial trickeries of distribution atonable and good.

"Your mind had to be tormented and fevered and exalted before you could see a god," is said somewhere in "In the Land of Youth." It is a strange book; to make it fashionable among some of the moderns we might call it a fantasy of miscegenation between two worlds—that of the gods and that of men (or Irishmen anyhow). And those that find it unreadable will be, I suppose, the lucky ones. Certainly no writer can afford to read it unless he is very stout-hearted; for he will find in it the music, the laughter, the simplicity, the bare and evasive truth, that he himself probably missed in a soapsud of words. Luminous as crystal, it gathers light around it until it shines with a brightness of its own; a brightness pure and unpurposeful enough to show how dark the world is.

Jamie Comes to Hy-Brasil

If Mr. Stephens was welcomed, as he should have been, by a file of publishers in shackles; and if, as he would, he then struck the irons from their ankles and greeted them with some merry redeeming word; and if they then repaired to various telephone boxes to order a resumption of the precessions of the press, well and good. If he was not so welcomed, I don't know what to suggest, except that I am willing to show him my private cathedral. From this secret eyrie where I hide and write I look out upon the great piers of the Brooklyn Bridge. They are pierced by tall lancet openings, that look, in the pearly East River air, like vast cathedral windows. There are two of these empty windows at each end; and between them rises my imagined cathedral. Of its creed or its various architecture I have nothing to say; of its shadowy tablets— whether to Walt Whitman or to Charles Edward Montague, or whoever—I do not now speak. But it would be pleasant to take Mr. Stephens down the aisle of that intangible minister, and to let him hear the organ sounding in honour of the unknown god, who disciplines no parishes and no sects; the god who now and then allows great poetry to be written. I should lay near the altar a copy of "In the Land of Youth," and say to Mr. Stephens:

"So came Jamie to Hy-Brasil."

LITTLE JOURNEYS

I HESITATED before raising the blind, for this was
going to be a Moment. I wanted to get the full
taste of it. The lower berth was comfortable, I had
found a diagonal position that eluded the usual hump
in the middle. I had slept well, after some midnight
twinges of laughter with "The Constant Nymph"; I had
arranged clothes and toothbrush and razor in careful
order where they would be easily at hand. I didn't
know exactly what time it was: presumably there had
been a change in the clock, but was it earlier or later
than my watch? At any rate, the thought of grape-
fruit was present. And now, to-day, I was to look for
the first time on the reality behind two great names—
names of romance since my boyhood. Ohio . . .
Indiana . . . what lovelier words are there?

Little Journeys

I raised the blind. It was a mild, pearly morning: a pale haze lay over wide fields softly silvered with dainty frost. A little grey farmhouse stood among trees, with a barn that asked me to chew MAIL POUCH. A tract of corn stubble dipped down toward a pond, and some small roan pigs were snouting about. It felt like Winesburg, it was as lovely as a dream. I remembered Sherwood Anderson's "Tandy." I knew that Anderson had told the truth, as poets usually do. Perhaps they are the only people you can depend on for the truth. Even the suburbs of Columbus could not dismay me after that first glimpse. I thought of O. Henry in prison in Columbus, and I thought of Omar Khayyám making his first American appearance in that city. On the fences of Xenia I saw bills for "Abie's Irish Rose."

But it is Indiana, not Ohio, that is the burden of my song. How can one decently impart a first impression of Indianapolis? Its very name, so pleasant an amalgam of two different kinds of suggestion (the red man and the Greek) seems to imply its lovable mixture of old-fashioned gentility with our modern pang. Nowhere have I had the happiness to meet such beautiful old ladies, ladies whom one adored at sight and who almost made one wish one might have been young fifty years ago. Could one forget, then, that it was in Indiana that Owen founded his New Harmony when all the world was young? Could one forget that so many poets have found in Indiana glades and valleys a sort of Theocritus voice of pastoral music? There was a perambulating supper held in the statuary hall of a big art museum. Underneath a huge figure of a horse, as big as the Trojan quadruped, tall candles burned on a long table and people in evening dress moved about with salad and coffee. There was a gentleman there who knew Austin Dobson by heart. I don't quite see how to convey what is in my mind, but one had a feeling that these gracious people had kept more closely in touch with the beauty of the past than many of our seaboard wits. It was at Bloomington that I heard the liveliest praise of Tennyson that I have lately encountered; and in a second-hand store in Indianapolis I found Fitzgerald's "Euphranor," which I had long hunted in vain in New York. This second-hand bookshop, incidentally, is conducted with Cromwellian rigour: the proprietor refuses admission to any mere browser, and ejects the customer who does not know exactly what book he wants.

Of course, it is absurd to try, on a basis of a few days' skirmish, to set down any memoranda of a way of living. We none of us know what civilization means, or where it is headed; even the great express trains (with half-a dozen new dictionaries in the club and observation cars to help the passengers solve their cross-word puzzles) utter a voice of strangely uncertain melancholy and defiance. But there are pictures in my mind that seem typical of that city's just and serene temper. On the front door of the Indianapolis Public Library you read the words "Friendly Books Welcome You." I think the delightful librarian was a little shocked when I ventured that all books are not friendly: for some of them indeed are dangerous and savage. But no books

could be as friendly as are the Indianapolitans themselves. There was an evening when a dozen or more of
us sat round the fire and played Twenty Questions
and charades and Intelligence Tests. I think it would
have been hard to find, that particular evening, a more
innocently hilarious gathering anywhere. In the Intelligence Test the visitor (he might as well admit it)
came far down the list of scores. Indianapolis, as befits
her reputation as a midwestern Athens, keeps nibbling
away at culture. It pleases me to think that one
charming lady I met is to read, this week, a paper on
Rhythm at her club; and Frank Wicks's Unitarian
Church is having an evening with Francis Thompson.
That church, which is one of the most genuinely inspir-
ing places I have ever seen, has almost the atmosphere
of a living room in an old English country house. There
is a smoking room for men in the basement, and the
windows, instead of haloed saints, are stained with a
design representing the foliage of the Tree Ygdrasil.
They sing hymns as though they really meant them,
and it is as though the company met for a house-party
with God. I remember the phrase "the heavenly
host."

In this church I heard the soloist singing "I will
lift up mine eyes to the hills," and wondered—a little
irreverently—what hills? for I hadn't seen any thereabouts. But then Percy Beach, the indefatigable book-
seller, drove me over to Bloomington and we saw a lovely
rolling country with bronze valleys and hillsides, a
cardinal bird flashing like a song escaped from some
anthology, and more of those lively russet-coloured

pigs. In the big courthouse square at Martinsville a buggy and a white horse were standing in the rain. But, greatest thrill of all, the first thing we saw in Bloomington was a poster announcing a Grand Old Time Fiddlers' Contest. "Sew Your Buttons on Tight and Prepare to Laugh." The Grand Capital Prize was to be "Choice of $25 Suit or Overcoat to Fit." And all the stores seemed to be offering special prizes. Faris Bros., meat market, "1 strip of Bacon to fiddler playing Saint Patrick's Day in the Morning, best." Fred W. Rumple "1 gallon red pitted cherries to best fiddler playing Money Musk." College Ave. Motor Co. "1 gallon can Veedol Oil to best fiddler keeping time with his feet." Walk-Over Boot Shop "1 pair woolen hose to best jews harp player." Uncle John's Cabin "2 pumpkin pies to fiddler playing Listen to the Mocking Bird." Siscoe Bros. "1 lady hair cut to longest bobbed hair girl contestant." Lem Howard "1 30 x 3½ tube to fiddler coming the farthest in a car." Fun in Big Bunches; Doors open at 7:00 P. M., says the bill, and "Explosion Takes Place at 8:00 F. M." Meredith Nicholson tells us in "The Hoosiers" that these fiddling contests were an old Indiana institution, but apparently they are rare nowadays. The manager of the theatre told me that he did not expect many of the college students to be interested in it; but I feel sure that it must have been an occasion as full of the real juices of life as the Cotter's Saturday Night.

The students of Indiana University—if their most intellectual review can be trusted—hanker for more cerebral explosions. "We need," cries an editorial,

Little Journeys

"for either a year's residence or a series of lectures, the kind of gigantic thinker who would be kicked out of most colleges—a James Harvey Robinson, a Meiklejohn, a Bertrand Russell, a Lewisohn, or a Havelock Ellis." Unterrified youths, they demand (in italics) "*a supreme artist in the realm of ideas.*"

It would be interesting to ponder a little about this. The chief embarrassment of college life is not too few ideas, but too many: Joseph Conrad has insisted that the world as we know it rests on some very old and simple notions; myself I think (again I gather my evidence chiefly from the undergraduate magazines I pored over in the train) that some of our friends have been painfully unsettled by biting off a whole meal of ideas at once. The winged Eros, for instance, seems to be riding them with a cruel spur. When they are just a little older they will be more cautious before deliberately encountering an idea, alone in a dark night. Before you invite a Gigantic Thinker into your family circle it may be well to consider whether you have earned him. If only those who have been ejected from other colleges will do, Shelley and Thoreau will give one enough to sharpen the teeth. I cannot quite believe that the undergraduate epoch is a ripe one for settling all the controversies of current argument. Perhaps at college is the time to enjoy a little innocent tranquillity.

IN ITALICS

I SHALL make a botch of what I'm about to say, because I fear the vibration that is in my mind is not quite conveyable. But anyhow, the rain sopping on the little balcony outside my window, and the look-off over Manhattan's cliffs, and the card here beside me, all make the attempt irresistible.

I have just discovered Italy. I know that in the eyes of cultivated readers I am going to be ridiculous; but that doesn't matter. I'll be honest with you. Since a certain rainy day in the summer of 1912—a day when it rained just as it is raining now, and I sat in a hotel in Basel and decided it was too wet to bicycle over the Alps—I had said to myself (subconsciously, not aloud, where I could be overheard) that I could get along without Italy. I said to myself that there

In Italics

were already too many things in the world to be
thought about, and that I'd have to sacrifice some of
them. I had America to think about, and England,
and Germany, and France; and then, later on, getting
married and earning a living and raising a family; and
I fell in love with Manhattan, and (in a kind of shame-
faced way) I said to myself that the new Cunard Building was probably a perfectly adequate substitute for
Italy. . . .

And then to-day, coming into the office quite un-
suspecting any staggering blow, there was that postcard on A. L.'s desk.

It's no use trying to describe that card to you, though
I'll tell you enough so that you can identify it. Underneath the picture is written FIRENZE, Cappella Riccardi
—Viaggio dei Magi—Un Cavaliere—Dettagli—Benozzo Gozzoli. The picture is of a young fellow in a
white embroidered cloak, with a crown and long curly
hair, riding on a white horse. He is accompanied by
spearmen. In the background is a very consciously
sculpturesque rocky hillside, a man galloping on horse-
back with lifted spear, and a couple of those very
capersome greyhounds loved by Renaissance artists.
These are pursuing the hindquarters of a flitting quadruped who has very nearly escaped, for his front half
has got right off the postcard. If the man on horse-
back doesn't hurl his spear quickly the venison will get
away. The white horse on which the protagonist is
riding is (as they say in art catalogues) richly capari-
soned; he is lifting his right front knee with the jol-
liest enthusiasm and pride; under his belly is visible

[201]

another dog, of a quite mongrellish sort, who (this is only our guess) has attached himself to the procession on his own hook and is enjoying himself greatly. The pricker of the rider's spur comes just over our mongrel's head and looks like a star honouring him.

Now this, I am painfully aware, gives no impression at all of the picture. And indeed, if the loveliness of the scene were transmissible in words, why should Benozzo Gozzoli have painted it? I only mention these details in order to enable connoisseurs of these matters to identify the thing and give them the pleasure of smiling at my simplicity. A. L., I learned, keeps this card on her desk to remind her that "beyond the Alps lies Italy." And I have borrowed it from her for a day or so until I can find some art dealer who can sell me a small photo of the thing.

For if this is what Italy means, I said to myself as I went through the curious adventures of a rainy day among those downtown cliffs—which included lunching with a pensive mandarin beside a window on the thirty-eighth floor and looking off at pyramids and pinnacles whorled in sifting mist and rain while we plotted a little innocent sorcery together—if this is what Italy means, it is high time that (in the charming phrase of the land) I "met up" with her. Of course it is true that I had once before, lunching aboard the steamship *Giulio Cesare* and tasting *asti spumante*, had a vague suspicion that Italy and I would get on well together. But, remembering my disappointment on that wet day in Basel, I had always said sternly, No, I can get along without her. Well, a wet day divided us; now a wet day has brought us together again. Then (how divine is chance!) in came Hugh Western, the Chicago sonneteer. Hugh is a student of Italian art; I broached my naïf excitement to him and showed him the postal card. When he saw it, a flash—like a flicker of spiritual lightning—went over his serene, well-bred features. That was enough. Gozzoli, evidently, was an old friend of his. And if Gozzoli could kindle that look of understanding on the face of a Chicago sonneteer, then, by heaven, Gozzoli is the man for me. Look here, I said to A. L., I'm going to write a letter to this fellow Gozzoli. She didn't quite perceive, and began to explain that Gozzoli . . . Never mind, I said, I'm going to write him a letter. And one of these days I shall.

The youth, the glamour, the enchantment, the shining witness of life as it needs must be lived, emanate from that painting so strongly as to change and fortify the whole current of a man's day. That white horse with its gallant rider—one of the Medicis, A. L. told me—moved invisibly before me all day. I trod in his company. I was the yellow dog that joined the parade; there I was, under his horse's belly, but the star-point of his spur glistened over my humble head. And even here in this cruel and magnificent city, I said to myself, life can yet be made noble and proud by art. A.L. begged me to get hold of some books and read up about the Medicis and Gozzoli; but I don't believe I want to. I prefer to imagine them, until I can lay eye upon the painting itself. A mural, she said. One of those things they paint on walls, I suppose, to prove that there are no walls.

The Romany Stain

I wish Benozzo Gozzoli could have seen the view I
see now as I am typing this. The thousand golden
panes of the Hudson Terminal, the Tel and Tel, and the
lesser buildings between, shining through the dusk and
wet; the dark little chapel and graveyard below; the
winged statue dim against the heavy grey sky. Bless
him, the man who did that horse's mild proud eye and
curly nostril, the petulant, snobbish, and yet almost
girlishly lovely face of young De Medici, Esq., the man
who knew how to give those spears just the right angle
of slant and the mongrel dog exactly his correct simper
of idiotic fool satisfaction—that man would have known
what to do about Downtown Manhattan at night. For
what are we to do about it? How are we, in this burning and maddening civilization, to recapture that almost
insolent glory of artistic fecundity? How shall we
"like pelicans from sore-tweaked bosoms feather a nest
for some great egg of song"?

That evening I broke the law.

EVERY TUESDAY

E VERY Tuesday," wrote John Donne in one of his
weekly letters to his friend Goodyer, "I make
account that I turn a great hour-glass, and consider
that a weeks life is run out since I writ. But if I aske
my self what I have done in the last watch, or would do
in the next, I can say nothing; if I say that I have
passed it without hurting any, so may the Spider in
my window."

And this came to me with a shock (it is the splen-

dour of Donne that almost everything he wrote comes
to you with a crash of recognition) because it was precisely my own case. For it is Tuesday evening that I
had set aside in my budget of Time for writing the
weekly Bowling Green. Though I never manage to get
at it until Wednesday forenoon, just before the printer
is expecting his copy. Tuesday evening, when one
knows that the Green is debit, so becomes the most
fertile of the week for something else. It becomes the
best of Shroves.

The revival of interest in Donne, gathering undercurrent for several years, now is unquestionable. Two
new books about him, this winter alone; and in "Elizabeth's" just-published novel, "Love," I find one of her
characters busy reading Donne and hankering to talk
about him. In such brilliant poets as Elinor Wylie
and John Crowe Ransom I seem to observe a voice
that the Dean would have understood. It is plain
that there is something in Donne that speaks to our
present time.

I am an incapable porter of such explosive baggage
as John Donne's writings. A little flash of him goes
me a long way. Even books about him carry the same
difficult voltage, so that I dip into them rather than
ponder through. But in Hugh Fausset's "John Donne:
A Study in Discord," though I have not traversed it all,
I found suggestions that led me toward private analogies valuable to myself. Mr. Fausset, in his lively excitement about Donne, wanders into some phrases
that struck me as indiscreet (e.g., "the rhythm of sense
plays a costive counterpoint upon the fluid rhythm of

sound")—but a man can hardly dig deeply into Donne
without becoming a bit arrant. The important thing
is that Mr. Fausset does convey the sense that in
Donne's pages "a great prince in prison lies." I always think of Donne, in his ecclesiastic robes, as Bag-
heera the black panther—beautiful in eloquence and
latent ferocity; and carrying, under his dark fur, the
bare callous of the old chain—the king's palace at
Oodeypore. A "baffled centaur" is Mr. Fausset's
happy description of him at one angle of his life.

Mr. Fausset thrillingly enumerates Donne's P's and
Q's—mostly P's, as his account is quartered into The
Pagan, The Penitent, The Pensioner, The Preacher.
Of the Pagan label (I must look up that word: didn't
it mean, originally, only a suburbanite—a commuter?)
I think Donne would have relished William James's
reply: "Don't call me a pagan: it sounds too sectar-
ian." For there was all Heaven and hell in him, and
a heat that dissolves the gum on any paper *affiche*.
Mr. Fausset gloriously quotes, as description of Donne's own way with a quill, his wildly humorous account
of the literary style of the Holy Ghost:

The Holy Ghost is an eloquent Author, a vehement,
and an abundant Author, but yet not luxuriant; he is
far from a penurious, but as far from a superfluous style
too.

Donne was a fountain filled with blood and ink. The
only man who ever lived, perhaps, who could have
written us an Old Testament measurably substitutional
for the Jacobite, had that been lost. Give us a modern

Donne and we will listen to these 20th century versions of the Bible. No lesser maniac will serve.

There was something Spanish in him. Mr. Fausset rather quaintly ascribes his sensuality to his Welsh blood; but his interest in Spain, from his childhood on, seems significant. Certainly there is something suggestive in the old legend—I don't know how old it may be; I invented it this minute—that Spain is the country where God lives. He lives there because He daren't turn His back on it; it is the weakest link in his chain of beads; there, if anywhere, He and the Demiurge will eventually "have it out." The most eloquent of our modern Satanophils have had a pinch of Iberia in them. At any rate Donne, like any sagacious Freudian, showed his passionate interest in Spain by going to war on her, in naval expeditions. That he was heartily seasick we know from his use of nauseous metaphor in later verse. But there was a Spain in his heart, and a Grand Inquisitor.

He is as modern, I think, as Sherwood Anderson; in fact, Mr. Anderson's washing-machine manufacturer —whom Mr. Anderson's fine imagination has long since transcended; for obvious reasons I do not say out-stripped—would have found much in common with Donne's frenzies. But even in his agonized third dec-ade, Donne retained the redeeming buoyancy familiar to washing machines. He was the Ninety and Nine of the hymn, and also the Forty Four One Hundredths. He floated. It is about all we can say.

Perhaps one reason why Donne is so inscrutably familiar, so couth and canny to our present generation of vipers, is that he did succeed in bruising the serpent with his heel. He learned, or almost we might say invented, the stunning truth that Man, the experimental artist, makes his greatest success when he plays over the head of his audience. Man's audience, of course, is Nature; and Nature, like any other audience, likes to feel that she is being given a Message; something that she (as they say at the ladies' clubs) "can take away with her." If you sing Mammy madrigals to her, she fills the house with automatic applause; but when you give her (as Donne did, from the pulpit of St. Paul's) the thrill of insane poetry, she listens in that uneasy awe and silence that is her best tribute to man.

I don't quite understand what Mr. Fausset means when he says that Donne "was neither a graceful nor a witty correspondent." To my taste his letters are the indivisible election of wit and grace. Mr. Charles E. Merrill edited some years ago the "Letters to Severall Persons of Honour." In there, together with much more stately matter, you will find a little series of letters "To the worthiest Lady Mrs. Bridget White." They make me perfectly understand the Dean's skill with ladies. Apparently Mistress Bridget, who was only in her teens, was not very punctual in reply. After several unanswered sorties Donne writes:

MADAME,

I have but small comfort in this letter; the messenger comes too easily to me, and I am too sure that the letter shall be delivered. All adventures towards you should be of more difficulty and hazard. But perchance I need not lament this; it may be so many of my letters are lost already that it is time that one should come, like *Jobs* servant, to bring word that the rest were lost. If you have had more before, this comes to aske how they were received; and if you have had none, it comes to try how they should have been received. It comes to you like a bashfull servant, who, though he have an extreme desire to put himself in your presence, yet hath not much to say when he is come. . . . Your going away hath made *London* a dead carkasse. A Tearm and a Court do a little spice and embalme it, and keep it from putrefaction, but the soul went away in you: and I think the onley reason why the plague is somewhat slackned is because the place is dead already, and no body left worth the killing.

Your humblest and affectionatest servant
J. D.

Surely no woman could resist this. Nor could any God resist Donne's sermons.

BERTHA AND HER POTTAGE

O F COURSE there must have been others also for
whom the word *Brooklyn* has always been a gram-
arye and a spell.   Probably it was Walt Whitman who
long ago cast a magic over that name, so that not
Stratford, Stoke Poges, Weimar, Valley Forge, Walden
—not even Cockeysville, Md., where the Sherwood
rye used to be distilled—none of the traditional shrines
had a livelier music in my skull.   Since then some of
the most unawaited excitements have transpired for

me in that borough which Mr. Lawton Mackall un-
gallantly called the butt end of Long Island. And my
actual entry into Brooklyn is demurely associated with
what I thought was the discovery of the amazing literary merit of Bertha M. Clay. (I wonder what the M.
stood for?)

It was a day, then, much like this; a drowsy forenoon
of early spring; and calm Brooklyn byways whose
names I have forgotten, perhaps they had none, lay
mild and yellow. I had been sent by a publishing house
to collect information, for publicity purposes, about one
of its authors who had died. The author (I can see
very plainly the picture of him we used again and again
—it was the only one we had—in our broadsheets sent
out to the press; his moustache was finely waxed) was
an Englishman, but he had a kinsman who lived in
Brooklyn. From this kinsman, a veterinary surgeon,
I was to glean some biographical details. It is a bit
vague in my mind, but I remember that near the house
was a stable or some sort of quadruped dispensary and
the doctor and I sat in a pleasant whiff of strong nostra
and horse. There was a glass of beer somewhere in
the picture, very cool and pleasant beer, blonde like
so much of Brooklyn's charm, and in the conversation
I learned that the vanished author had been one of those
who wrote the novels signed with the great name of
Bertha M. Clay.

This may or may not have been exact; but young
men in the publicity professions are not gruesomely
concerned with doctrines on the fallibility of human
transmission. In any case it was a good "item" and

Bertha and Her Pottage

I knew that my boss would be pleased. And I resolved to make the acquaintance of Miss Clay's works.

This was not immediately easy, but one day I found myself in the neighbourhood of Ninth Avenue and Twenty-eighth Street (Manhattan). This time I believe I was on some errand for the editor of the *Garden Magazine*, something to do with a flower show, and the wholesale florists were along West Twenty-eighth. You have no idea, incidentally, how many quaint errands are devised to keep active and alert the young apprentices of the publishing business. In a stationery shop on Ninth Avenue I found a fine display of Bertha Clays. I bought one, perhaps "The Shadow of a Sin" or "Thrown on the World," though I admit that Charles Garvice and Charlotte Braeme had more skill in titles. Why didn't I buy "Neither Maid, Wife, nor Widow"? The title has haunted me ever since. For the conclusion was irresistible, she must have been a Cartesian, as Mr. Clem Hawley would say. In that region there is a park, whose name escapes me; and there I sat on a bench reading my first Bertha Clay. I rapidly came to the conclusion that it was dull twaddle and left it on the seat.

We now skip several years. One evening, in a ten-cent store in Hempstead, L. I., I found a lot more Bertha Clays and determined to have another try. The volume I chose, at random, was "A Dead Heart"; The Arthur Westbrook Company, Cleveland, U. S.A., publishers; postage stamps taken the same as money. "A Dead Heart" was there, sure enough, but it was followed by another tale printed in much larger type, and I tackled the second one first. By the time I had read three or four paragraphs I got up from the couch in excitement. I've done Bertha an injustice, I said. There's something to her after all. Why, she's kidding them!

The story was about a young Scot, a graduate in theology and logic (only a Scot could graduate in both these simultaneously) who went to London to look for a job. He wanted to be private secretary to a member of the Cabinet and "if time permitted he proposed writing for the press." He says good-bye to his Scotch sweetheart. "Andrew did not open the door for her, for he was a Scotch graduate. Besides, she might one day be his wife." The girl is briefly described. "Clarrie was beautiful and all that." Their parting:

Andrew stooped and kissed her upturned face.
"If a herring and a half," he said anxiously, "cost three halfpence, how many will you get for elevenpence?"
Clarrie was mute.

With growing enthusiasm I continued. Andrew, the hero, goes to London.

It was the first time he had set foot in England, and he naturally thought of Bannockburn.

Mr. Gladstone and Mr. Chamberlain were too busy to see him, and he became embittered. He tried journalism:

He sent one of the finest things that was ever written on the Ontology of Being to paper after paper, and it

was never used. He threatened the *Times* with legal
proceedings if it did not return the manuscript.

The *Standard* sent him somebody else's manuscript,
and seemed to think it would do as well.

A certain amazement was taking hold of me as I
scoured through these witty pages. Good heavens,
here was Bertha Clay, whom I had regarded as a mere
caterer of plum duff, turning off this graceful and high-
brow burlesque. I felt I owed Bertha an apology.

Andrew was reduced to rereading his testimonials
for consolation. He had a sheaf of them, from the
Rev. Peter Mackay of Dundee and many other Scottish logicians and divines:

Had you met him in the Strand conning them over,
you might have taken him for an actor. He had a
yearning to stop strangers in the streets and try a
testimonial's effect on them.

He had two pounds with him when he came to London, and in a month they had almost gone.

He took to writing obits:

When the newspaper placards announced the serious
illness of a distinguished man, he made up characteristic
anecdotes about his childhood, his reputation at
school, his first love, and sent them, as the reminis-
cences of a friend, to the great London dailies. These
were the only things of his they used. As often as not,
the invalid got better, and then Andrew went without
a dinner.

In his despair our Andrew joins the S. D. W. S. P.
—the Society for Doing Without Some People—and
earns a modest living by helping to assassinate public

figures who have proved wearisome to the members of
this excellent club. The only personages exempt from
possible removal are those who have been elected honorary members. The first man of any note that
Andrew dispatched with his own hands was "*Punch's*
favourite artist on Scotch matters." He was on the
track of the man who signs himself *Paterfamilias* in
letters to the *Times*. To his great pleasure he learned
that "none of these American preachers who come
over to this country are honorary members."

Well, as you see, by this time I felt it was too good to
be true. I was carrying Bertha Clay round with me
and expounding her as an unappreciated satirist. I
went in to see a connoisseur of such matters. "Have
you ever read Bertha Clay?" I asked. "She's immense." I read him some of it.

"What's it called?" he asked.

"It's called 'Better Dead,' it's the second story in
this book 'A Dead Heart.' The great thing about
Bertha seems to be her versatility. It's totally different
from the first story."

"Bertha Clay!" he shouted. "'Better Dead'?
Why, you fathead, do you know what that is? It's
Barrie's first book, published in '88. This is probably
the first American edition, pirated. Darned valuable
as a curiosity. Can you get me a copy?"

I went back to the ten-cent store. The counter
where Bertha had reigned was devoted to Easter eggs.

"I'm sorry," said the young woman, "they were
taken off sale last week. There's not much call for
literature here."

Bertha and Her Pottage

But I often wonder what the readers of "A Dead Heart" can possibly make of that little skit of Barrie's when they find it masquerading under the name of Bertha M. Clay. And in the same volume, at the very end (just before the advertisement of "Napoleon's Oraculum"), you'll find a yarn called "My Own True Ghost Story," written by a young man in Allahabad. But that also goes in as one of Bertha's. I begin to understand why so many people, including the Arthur Westbrook Company, regard Bertha as a great writer.

STORMS AND CALMS

EVERY now and then there bobs up—not undiscouraged by the ingenious publishers—some argument as to the order in which the reader should "approach" Conrad's works. In a recent symposium "20 Famous Critics Tell Readers How To Start Reading Joseph Conrad's Books." To a publisher all critics are famous, just as in the dark all cats are grey. But the interesting thing to me is to observe the majority by which these old salted Conrad shellbacks advise the apprentice to begin with what Conrad himself called his "storm pieces"—"Youth," "Typhoon," "The Nigger." It reminds me that Shakespeare's storm piece, "The Tempest," is always put first in his collected editions. I wonder why?

I am not deposing any thesis; I am merely wondering. I suppose the most rational way of reading any man's work, and the most arduous, is in the chronology of its writing; so can you trace the course of his mind. But only serious students are likely to do that; most readers are more haphazard. And I have an affectionate disrespect for those who will allow their dealings with so fascinating an author as Conrad to be too much dictated by what critics suggest.

I wonder, though, whether Conrad did not have a very particular tenderness for what he has called his "calm pieces"; and whether, for many readers (who find hurricane and breaching seas genuine vertigo to soft head and stomach), "'Twixt Land and Sea" and "The Shadow Line" are not a more tactful beginning? Of course, it is easier to admire storm pieces than calms; perhaps also easier to write them (I am not asserting; only wondering; nothing great is easy to write, I have been told). But I am often faintly surprised that in talk about Conrad one hears so little of "The Shadow Line" and the three tales in "'Twixt Land and Sea." In the case of a man like Conrad I think you have to watch him carefully for his most significant utterances; and when he says casually in the preface to "The Shadow Line," "I admit this to be a fairly complex piece of work," perhaps he covertly means, "This is a devil of a big thing if you have the wit to discern it." At any rate, it *is* a devil of a big thing; and if one considers the time when it was written (the closing months of that gruesome year 1916) it takes place as one of the most heroic achievements in a not easy life. In that story there is a sudden picture of a seaman at the ship's wheel at night, his brown hands on the spokes lit up in the darkness by the glow of the binnacle. I will not spoil your pleasure in the picture by insisting on the symbolism that Conrad intended; he explains it himself in the tale; and perhaps one of his weaknesses was that of too often explaining symbolism. But the bronze-shining hands on that shadowy wheel, the ship becalmed, the anxious question "Won't she answer the helm at all?"—these are matters for as careful meditation as the Chinese coolies battered to and fro in the hold of the *Nan-Shan*. When Conrad gave "The Shadow Line" its subtitle, "A Confession," when he hoisted on its halliards that quotation from Baudelaire, he was doing something that deserves watching.

It is foolish of me to write about Conrad; and certainly I should never try to prejudice readers in favour of trying one special book before another. There are several Conrads that I have never read myself; perhaps I never shall. Up to the present I have as much of him under hatches as I can properly stow. I have, I think, much the same feeling that he had when he came up New York harbour in the *Tuscania*. After a long and very careful study of that skyline he retreated to the port wing of Captain Bone's bridge and averted his eyes. He had had all he could carry.

But, since none of the present symposiarchs seem to have mentioned them, I can't help saying a word about the extraordinary stories in "'Twixt Land and Sea." "The Secret Sharer," is it a magnificent allegory of the horrors of man's duality? Of course, it doesn't matter whether you believe it is or not; like all great fables the suggestion is so implicit that as soon as you try to define it you destroy it. There indeed is the trouble to which all writers of fable are victim: when you ask them exactly what they mean, you murder them. If the "moral" of the thing can be explained, it is vanished. It can only be felt. Take the case of another story in the same book, "A Smile of Fortune." There is some colossal irony lurking in the thing; but after perhaps half a dozen readings in the past ten years, I would not venture to graph it. Is Jacobus, the thick-lipped ship chandler, offered to us as a veiled hero or as a scoundrel eager to traffic in the allure of his bastard daughter? And the girl herself, can you tell me any more wretchedly pitiable prisoner, yet how her terror and slattern beauty and potential vitality haunt us from those dead pages. What does it all simmer down to in the end? A deal in potatoes —the potatoes that Jacobus "paraded" (glorious word!) on the table. Any one who would ask what that story "means" is absurd. It means just what to-day means, and yesterday, and a week from next Thursday.

I imagine (I'm only wondering, not asserting) that perhaps the men best fitted to relish Conrad, the men who have known something of the life he describes and are also brooders on the interwoven toe and heel of destiny, are most likely to turn to his "calm pieces" for that enveloping haze of significance which is his greatest gift. An extraordinary duplicity of meaning shimmers in those tales; the slightest movement becomes heavy ("fraught," the reviewers would say) with omen. It is in such stories that he recurs to his favourite theme of the great security of that old sea life as compared with the unrest and fever of the land. Happy, happy man, who through the most difficult years of manhood could mature himself in that hard

and mannerly calling—"that untempted life present-
ing no disquieting problems, invested with an elementary moral beauty by the absolute straightforwardness
of its appeal and by the singleness of its purpose."
Exempt from false sophistication and ethical jugglery,
exempt from cultivated palaver, he was free to deepen
himself in that beautiful naïveté which all great poets
must have.   He became, one thinks, almost as naïf as
Keats or Shakespeare, with a heart as open to moral
simplicities, to honest and ironic sentiment, to simple
humours that could even make their mirth over a pair
of whiskers.   Then, like the secret sharer, he "lowered
himself into the water to take his punishment: a free
man, a proud swimmer striking out for a new destiny."

So I am wondering.   I am wondering whether there
isn't something in (for example) "The Shadow Line"
that makes even "Typhoon" or "Youth"—yes, even
"Heart of Darkness"—seem a trifle melodramatic?
These great things, and heaven knows they *are* great,
are so precisely what the literary critics *would* most
admire.   But somehow, hidden away between the
lines, I feel more of the essential agony in "The Shadow
Line" and "The Secret Sharer."   I haven't even mentioned "Freya," the third story in "'Twixt Land and
Sea"—that desolately tragic tale that tells (if you
choose to interpret it so) what happens to beautiful
things when they run up against "authorities."   These
are all calm-water stories, laid in the luxurious Eastern
sunshine that (Conrad suggests) has more psychic cor-
ruption than the fiercest northern gale.   It is when
becalmed that the sailor has time to think.

THE CREATIVE LIFE

AFTER reading "The Dance of Life"* once, I
thought: how agreeable to sit down and write
copiously about it. After reading it twice, a more
decent humility prevails. To "review" Mr. Ellis's
fertile and fructuating book would be as impossible as
to review life itself. For it speaks to those interior
questionings and honesties where the happiest wisdom
is silence. Yet, for an action to be comely (Mr. Ellis
somewhere suggests) it need only be fitting to its particular relationships at its particular moment. The
relation that has grown up between this book and myself is such that I would feel cowardly not to testify.
And perhaps the man who has crowned his old age
by this noble résumé of a life's thinkings would find
no impropriety in a salute from a young ignoramus

*"The Dance of Life," by Havelock Ellis, Houghton Mifflin Co.

[223]

The Romany Stain

desperately but sincerely groping for those liberations of spirit that help to make life artful. It is by its echo in young and undisciplined hearts that Mr. Ellis's book will prove its virtue.

To make life artful. . . . It is living itself considered as an art that is the acorn of Mr. Ellis's foliage. Indeed, one has long suspected that the artists—using the word in no narrow sense—inkle truest happiness, for they have discarded (unconsciously, for the most part) the merely conventual and nonessential. Without the peace, the humility, the rigorous aversions, the charitable humours which we can learn from them, there is ill chance of our becoming more than mere botchers at this greatest of skills. Disobedience to the artistic instinct of the soul, its troubled but divinely judicious intuition of harmonies, is the most cruelly punished of human errors.

The dance of life! I have feared that to modern connotation Mr. Ellis's title may sound misleading: for the word *dance* has acquired slipshod and rowdy suggestions. The rhythms and measures he divines are more majestic and more obscure, more truly jocund yet also more tranquil, than those our mind is wont to image. One of the most beautiful things our time has invented is the slowed motion picture: just so we must conceive the pattern of the universe scanned on a scale that makes manifest its exquisite hesitation and pause. The recurring rondo of our joys and follies is a part of it, as much as the sprinkled movements of the sky. I was once one of a group of boys and girls that used to meet, in Oxford, to caper the old English country dances. In the rustic figures of "Jenny Pluck Pears" and "Gathering Peascods" and "Up Tails All," in "Dargason" ("or, The New Sedany"), and "Three Meet" ("or, The Pleasures of the Town"), accompanied by those adorable gay and wheedling old musics, we youthfuls frolicked in a merriment that was immortally harmless, hale, brimming with utter fun. In some unquestionable way one knew one's self attuned to the full meaning and melody of life. This was play —that is to say, art—at its most innocent best: I have never approached any happiness like it. When I remember the perfected charm and gusto of that jolly sport, whether indoors or on green lawns or damp riverside meadows, I realize what Mr. Ellis means when he suggests the primitive sensibility of the dance as the germ of all thought, all morals. So I beg for faith in the instinct of the true artist. That is sufficient for me: I am a solifidian.

But all advances in thought, as Mr. Ellis summons many testimonies to prove, are assisted by fictions. And this book itself, so full of brave encouragement, is, I daresay, fictive enough. For though he urges us to believe that perhaps the art-instinct is the *primum mobile* of the spirit world (just as some one element may be fundamental in all matter), yet we know ourselves too well to be over-hopeful. Is there any sensitive person who has not found himself continually hampered and thwarted in his justest impulses, calloused by the friction of competing hopes, crazed by the tragedy of needless and meaningless hastes and bickerings, thus tottering an errant course rather than proceeding with the clear sobriety of art? Civilization, though it often extorts our reluctant admiration, yet is also maddening. I have seen a New York taxi-driver, spinning his cab round a crowded corner, unconsciously roll his eyes with just the bewildered frenzy of a dog that isn't yet quite certain whether to bite or not. I have ridden in suburban electric trains where the continual crashing of metal doors, jarring of windows, jolting of starts and stops, racing of belated passengers to leap aboard at every station, all combined in a hullabaloo so shocking that unless one retired into a secret core of indifference one would surely go insane. Only too well we know our lives to be absurd and unwholesome; and we seek passionately, impossibly, to be made significant and whole.

These contradictions and paradoxes of life as we know it, Mr. Ellis patiently and generously considers. With the occasional sprinkle of bitterness that is palatable in philosophy, with the nicest simplicity of manner, and (more important still) with an eye cleansed by feasting on the wideness of Time and Space, he takes us through the four great arts that are most urgent to our condition: the art of Thinking, the art of Writing, the art of Religion, the art of Morals. Ever since I first encountered the book, I have wished there were some way of making it compulsory study for parsons. For though it gives little consolation to churches, it has profound energy for those who esteem religion as the noblest form of æsthetic.

The fiery particle will not be put off with quibble or evasion. It is, it *is* important and needful that one should at least try to live life as an art, that it should be exempt from pitiable hagglings and cowardly surrenders. And Ellis's special charm, perhaps, is that he keeps rediscovering to us those most precious of all secrets—our own thoughts, those we buried, forgot, or fled from in dismay. The notions we were a little leery of, that we folded neatly and hid under a stone while we went bathing in the clear swift stream of life, we here find again and recognize as the most important. His pages on the essential unity of science and art, for example. He insists that they are homoiousian (a word he does not use, but I do, for I love a good rollicking pedantry now and then). Those passages are the richest delight to any one who has been privileged to guess the imaginative poetical spirit that irradiates all genuine scientific inquiry. Everywhere he is on the side of the angels; and while he says very little that is novel or startling to any alert thinker, yet he says quite enough to galvanize many a merchant in intellectual hand-me-down and shoddy. And his substance is charmingly organized and thought out. The chapter on literary art is truism to any intuitive lover of language; yet how admirably and winningly put. Always we find him taking the cudgel against stultifying rule and rigidity, the picayune pettifogging spirit that would construe the text of life as a proof-reader corrects galley slips. In the "Art of Morals," for instance, how eloquently he buttresses every artist's contention (sure to be misunderstood, of course) that to the philosopher there is no such thing as "morality," as vulgarly apprehended; for morality ceases to exist when it becomes conscious. Morality, of course, is merely what is mannerly and customary: and Mr. Ellis frankly would have us all as "immoral" as Jesus was.

What, then, if we try to lay penpoint upon it, is the cardinal bearing of this great book? I think it is this, that each of us (if capable of thought at all; and he excellently insists that not all are so capable) is an artist creating his own truth from the phenomena life gives him. The kingdom of Heaven is within us indeed, and each must be his own Buddha, his own Christ, his own Leonardo. This dark and pricklesome necessity surely does not imply any relaxing of our imperilled responsibility, rather an all the more stringent devotion to our little ember of artistic conscience. Out of these fantastic intractable materials that life has poured about us we must compose our picture as best we may —like prisoners of war carving cunning toys of corncobs and peanut shells and chewing gum. Time— which is, I suppose, the canvas we paint on, the clay we knead—flows fast and faster—so fast, sometimes, we dimly suspect ourselves very close to the place it comes from. Every instant is an emergency, and we are apprenticed to the art of living before we know enough to have any choice. As so often on railroads, the brakeman doesn't call out the names of the stations until after the train has started. By the time we learn where we are going—it sounds very like Nothingness? —it is too late to cancel the ticket.

Any man who writes as plainly as Mr. Ellis of the real issues of life, is certain of a few sniffs and hoots. But he helps us toward the only task worth while, the only task that can bring us peace—the attempt to deal not as hucksters, but as poets, with the rough, blazing, infinitely precious fragments of life. He helps us to face the exquisite riddle with greater piety and courage, and to turn our necessity to glorious gain. Perhaps it is not inappropriate to say of his book, as he says of Lange's "History of Materialism" that so moved him years ago, "it can never be forgotten by any one who read it in youth."

POSTSCRIPT TO THE LOG

THAT morning the Nigger was first on deck. Behind Duck Island breakwater, where the *Narcissus* (a 41-foot ketch) had taken shelter the night before, it was quiet, warm, and hazy; but there was a kind of omen in the air. *7 A. M. Bar. 29.64—light breeze SSW* was the Nigger's entry in the rough log, for he was learning the laconic brevity esteemed in log books. But he mentioned his suspicions of the weather to the Skipper. The latter, by the simple act of putting on his cap, was ready for command: he had turned in all standing after a hard day.

The Nigger lit the fire and put on Charley Noble Senior to speed the draught. In sailing craft, as perhaps I don't need to tell you, the top section of the galley stovepipe, with its lateral vents to keep rain out of the fire and to catch the air at any slant of wind, is traditionally known as Charley Noble. But the spare cylinder of pipe, tall and open at the top, put on when a hot stove was needed in a hurry, we had honoured with the name of Noble Sire or Charley Noble Senior. (The two, collectively, were referred to as the Two Noble Kinsmen.) When the Skipper saw Noble Senior put on, his eye always brightened; this meant that victual was toward.

The Nigger would like to persuade himself it was that omen in the air that toughened the jam omelet. Jam omelet had been promised the Skipper for breakfast; the last half-dozen eggs (this was the fifth morning of the *Narcissus*'s cruise) had been saved for it. But he knows it was merely that he didn't beat them enough. The omelet was as tough as biltong, which heroes used to eat in Captain Mayne Reid's stories. But it was eaten in much peace: the *Narcissus*, under jib and mizzen, sailed herself gently out into the Sound, while the Skipper kept an eye on the tell-tale compass set beside him on the table.

A wonderful quiet morning, the light air gradually hauling to westward, a hazy pallor all round the horizon. In that widest stretch of Long Island Sound we were soon out of sight of land; no other craft was visible; we rippled softly in a great vacancy made all the more precious by faint foreboding that something was stirring in the far blue hollows of the weather. It grew so surprisingly hot that the Nigger wondered whether some of his warmth wasn't due to sunburn. The Skipper was overhauling gear in the forepeak. "Were you rumbling something down there?" asked the Nigger presently. The Skipper said No; so that almost inapprehensible rolling of weights, that soft shifting of huge volumes of air, must have been thunder. The glass kept pretty steady around 29.63 and .64; the Skipper enhanced the mid-ocean feeling of our shimmering solitude by getting out his sextant and shooting the sun. But a pleasant lethargy circled in our veins; the Skipper did not work out the position, contenting himself by narrating how once, passenger in S. S. *Tuscania* at sea, Captain David Bone had allowed him to take a noon observation from the bridge; but, rattled by the proximity of this famous navigator, the amateur misread his tables. When he presently announced his finding of *Tuscania's* position he had located her somewhere in the placid waters of Lake Sebago, Maine. At midday the *Narcissus* was softly dipping in a lucid calm. To put on some porridge to simmer was all the Nigger could persuade himself to achieve. He even forgot (and now remembers it with chagrin) to clean up the sticky place at the back of the grocery cupboard, where in the heavy rolling of the day before a tall marmalade jar, too loosely wedged, had toppled over and oozed a sirupy juice. Presently came a slant of breeze from NE and land was duly ho'd. This was Herod Point; and the name sounded threatening too.

So passed the warm divisions of early afternoon. A spell of airless silence, a breath of air from SE; another sleepy interim and a puff from ESE: the beguiling comedians of Aeolus seeking to distract their audience's attention from what was really preparing behind the backdrop. Only the boatman's ever-present necessity of something to be done kept the two from yielding to the torpor that was heavy in their legs. The Skipper got out his lead line and marked off fathom lengths with scraps of flannel. The Nigger finished a painting job that had been keeping him busy on the cabin roof. The dinghy was lashed a little more firmly to the deck. Both remarked the number of insects that came aboard: a ladybug, a wasp, and two or three other flitting midgets. Instead of blundering about for a moment or so and then winging away, as they usually do a few miles offshore, these creatures seemed disposed to crawl into corners and take cover. The Nigger found the wasp tucking himself into a niche in the very angle of the stem, between the bowsprit and the deck. Surely, he said to himself, this too is a sign of storm. He made sure that the porridge was well anchored on the stove, and sat to write up the log. In the pleasures of that task he was completely absorbed: his pipe was drawing well, the Skipper was ware and watchful at the wheel: for the time being, all portent and presage had vanished from his mind. It was eight minutes past four when the master called down "I think it's really coming." They hastened to get down the mainsail and stow away the painting job which had been drying on the cabin trunk. Just as the thick clouds let loose their rain—at 4:35, when commuters get ready to leave the office and make for the train; for all Long Island thunderstorms are justly calculated to catch the homeward traffic—a little school of porpoises came plunging almost alongside of us. When you see them from the tall deck of a liner you can't hear the snorting sneeze they make each time they emerge. They came close by on the starboard side, until we could see their little eyes catch sight of us: they dived under and vanished. Within the next hour, with drenching tattoos of rain, musketry of hail, and lively stripes of lightning, we were almost as wet as they.

Still, though there had been little puffs from all quarters, there had been no real wind. The Skipper by some overtrust of disposition had concluded that the Nigger was prescient in the matter of weather. "Do you feel as though there was going to be a hell of a blow?" he asked, with his customary copiousness of monosyllable. The Nigger, standing with only his head out of the companionway (for why, as he said, should they *both* get wet unnecessarily? and he was pretending to be engrossed at the galley), keeked warily about. True, the barometer had gone down to 29.54; and yet the Nigger, Lord forgive him, did not *feel* as though anything preternatural was brewing. A long, steadily pouring wet night was what he expected. Now, off Mount Misery (which you will find near Port Jefferson on the map) came a flavorous southeastern breeze. It was strong with all the odours of wet pine woods and dripping May earth. Only Long Island, exclaimed these two enthusiasts, could so tincture an air with whiffs of richness. The Nigger, still pondering the problem of getting into the narrow rulings of the logbook as much as possible, asked whether it would be too literary to note 5:50 *Mount Misery abeam. A beaker full of the warm South.* In this fresh and resiny current they laid their course West. Thunder and lightning seemed to have gone by. Even, at 6:45, all seeming propitious, they were wondering whether the mainsail might safely be raised again. At midnight, they were reckoning, they ought to make Glen Cove.

"If this one hasn't got wind in it, I never saw any," said the Skipper. His tone brought the Nigger instantly to the companion. In the northwest was a huge white raft of cloud, curiously whorled and voluted over itself, not unlike the downward curve of the water at Niagara's edge. Behind it was dark purple; under it, ink-black. There was just time to sling on an oil-skin coat and stand by the mizzen sheet. When it struck, carrying level shots of rain, this was no mere wind. It was a solid body, moving from somewhere to somewhere else at sixty miles an hour. The purple water was instantly ribbed with crisping parallels of silver, which, as soon as they were high enough, were whipped off in ragged membranes. Down to her lee rail *Narcissus* wallowed. The jibboom snapped: the jib, catching tons of pressure in that sharp angle, might well have gone to ribbons but didn't. Both, though they didn't admit it until later, waited to see the mast go; which would have meant the lee shore of Mount Misery a mile away. Why, was the first thought of the Nigger, as he sat on the weather gunwale up to his hams where the seas were creaming down from forward, Why did he name her *Narcissus?* She's going to do the same thing as Conrad's. I wonder which is more anxious in such moments: to be Skipper at the wheel, with the full responsibility; or to be Nigger hanging on to the weather stay, winking sluices of salt from your eyes and waiting to obey whatever orders may come. But, as the Skipper remarked, it can't blow like this very long. It did, though. Half an hour can be a long time. Of course you know that a solid bit of Maine boat-building won't turn turtle; and yet when you crawl into the cabin to look at the barometer after twenty minutes of hurricane, you rather expect her to go Jonesward as soon as you are below. The Nigger hasn't forgotten that barometer reading. It was 29.62. It had turned upward again. Nor did he ever know exactly how the potatoes that had been boiling on the stove got into the coal bin.

As Conrad quoted in his title-page motto for the original *Narcissus:*

My Lord discovered a great deal of love to this ship.

THE TONKA BEAN

THERE is a Great Caliph who lives in a castle by
the sea. This Arabian potentate, in the intervals
of his manifold affairs, has a specially ingenious form of
relaxation. He waves his wand and summons from
remote provinces parents who need a brief exemption
from family duty. Parents of young children are his
hobby: he Collects them, one might say; he installs
them in his turreted pavilion; he whispers to them
the magic phrase; and then he lights his pipe and
watches them enjoy themselves. This Caliph is, one
fears, a comfortable fellow. He uses tonka beans to
flavour his tobacco. He snuffs the steam of Darjeeling
tea as an asthmatic infant inhales Vapo-Cresoline.
And, like the tonka bean in his tobacco, so the amusement of watching other people being happy is an
aromatic capsule in his existence.

Not to be misunderstood, by the way, I will tell you
what are the magic words I alluded to. They are
two: *Room Service*. You go to a telephone and say
them gently. Shortly afterward high-spirited djinns
come brisking in, carrying portable tables. There is a

flourish of white linen, a musical chiming of silver dish covers, a vapor of hot viands. You sit, easily enough, watching the parallel confusions of the surf under the castle windows. It is not polite to talk with your mouth full, so, for a while, there is small speech.

A great adventure, certainly, for patres and matres familiæ, once a year or so, to flit briefly from the instant discipline of home. But Woman, I believe, relapses even more gently than Man into the felicity of sluggishness. Woman (I wish her luck, by the way) is natively a luxuriating animal. Man, or at any rate Man who has been trained as a commuter, has lost the accomplishment of lying late in the morning. But Woman, within the turning of one night, can placidly revise her whole schedule and snooze as beautifully as a half-tamed leopard. Meanwhile the pensive philosopher goes for a stroll, adding to his private collection of disbelievables and astonishments.

In the vast lobby, downstairs, with its flags and palms and café-au-beaucoup-lait pillars, its charming inverted mushrooms of electricity, he walks dreamily. Above a flight of stairs glimmers a great crystal sphere which has something of a magical hypnotic effect. There are great blocks of very dark green marble—almost black—which recall some story in the Arabian Nights where a number of people were turned, from the trouser-pocket down, into just such polished stone. Elevator boys, not quite so dark as that marble, have also something delightfully fairy-tale about them. They seem to have been translated by Burton. When the Room Service voice asks you over the 'phone,

The Tonka Bean

"American or European plan?" (always so startling a question, for we can never remember which is which; and Senators have dinned it into us that we must avoid European involvements), I always want to reply, Arabian Plan. That is the plan the office uses, anyhow, with all those Arabic numerals. I shouldn't wonder if the castle has 1001 rooms—or, as Burton would put it, a Thousand Rooms and a Room.

Atlantic City, or at any rate that special slice of it that I have been studying, is a community very truly infused with the spirit of art. To take the matter on its humbler level first, even the sand sculptors who shape Kiwanis and Rotary emblems on the beach, or the Lion of Lucerne, or shipwrecked mariners on a raft, even these craftsmen have a certain proud flash in the eye as they look up to the Boardwalk. Their signs say TO PRAISE I'M DIFFERENTIAL, BUT THE COINS ARE THE ESSENTIAL, or, more indirectly, REMEMBER THE ARTIST. Aye, indeed, let the Artist be Remembered. But a little opportunity to talk about his art is also very precious to him. It may be the borzoi-fancier at the Dog Show, combing out his long-nosed fragile silver-curly hounds before trotting them into the ring for judgment; or the maître-d'hôtel in the dining room, explaining why, of all the posts he has held in many famous houses, this is the one that most enlists his spirit; or (supreme honour) the Chef Himself, in his spotless linen coat and towering cap, showing some specially ornamented jellied meats—a glitteringly marbled thigh of pig on which is a spray of enchanting little flowers cut out of turnips, or a chicken on whose fair bosom we find stencilled a robin-redbreast, embossed of miraculously thin shavings of truffle and reddened with paprika. The Chef—it is no other than M. Elie Sivade—is happy to accept your honest homage, and with a touch of genuine pathos regrets that he cannot, now, enjoy himself by executing these details in person. His eye dwells approvingly upon a floral *décor* surmounting some galantine or other—the petals are of dainty spirals of tomato, the centre a thin wafer of lemon peel. But he can no longer, for the dignity of his position, perform those engaging divertissements himself. He invents, he directs, he instructs, he supervises: but the actual happy task is done by his apprentices. Perhaps that is one of the sadnesses of rising to the very top in one's art. Let us (we say to ourself) resolutely remain a little lower than the Summit.

The Caliph, as I said before, hides in his tobacco jar a few small black capsules—he calls them tonka beans —which impart to his mixture a pleasing moisture, fragrance, and pervasive gentle savour. At any rate, he says they do: and in matters of taste it is what you believe that matters. And so, like the buried tonka bean, this little secret of pride in his own work refreshes and perfumes the bosom of every genuine artist. This is the very essence of morale, that mysterious exhilaration that employers and college presidents and military commanders labour to inspire. It is just this genius for eliciting personal loyalty that some have thought the Deity, by too distantly absenting Himself from the scene, somewhat underrated. For the Deity must surely have realized that many problems could be

solved by an effective sublimation of Pride, that most
adorable and troublesome quality among His children.
For, if you are really proud of belonging to the human
race, you will be noblesse-obliged to pay judicious
deference to other sharers of that enigmatic honour.
We had no intention of dipping into metaphysic:
merely intended to say that all along the Boardwalk we
see the most agreeable panorama of human jauntiness
and self-esteem. Almost unavoidably one resolves to
be a little more of an Artist one's self. To keep one's
weight down to 180; to be a shade nicer in the gradation
of tint between shirt and necktie; to remember that
the people who iron trousers and dry-clean hats are
also eager to earn a living.

And I have discovered a Bank in which poets ought
to keep their accounts. For the sake of the bankers,
I would not limit its deposits to the checks received by
lyrists; but, joking aside, it deserves a paragraph of
its own. It is the new building of the Equitable Trust
Company in Atlantic City; a sober, secure, dignified
little edifice when first seen from the outside; then,
as you study it, unobtrusive charms begin to be ap-
parent. The cunningly rounded window-corners, the
marble strips inside the window-frames, the tall
columns of contrasting marble at the front door, leading
up to a porch ceiling of iridescent tiles which, when lit
at night, glitter like peacock feathers—all this is hand-
somely symbolic of the spirit of a city whose prosperity
is based upon gaiety—whose livelihood is liveliness.
And inside, if you are a lover of such matters, Mr.
Kelly, the delighted cashier, will show you how different

the building is from the dull heaviness or the equally dull magnificence of most successful banks. First, while the building had seemed not large, you will be amazed at the space and height: at the soft shining of the birch-bark coloured walls, the iron grill-work suggestive of old Spanish treasure chests, the touches of colour and harmony everywhere. Behind the iron railing the open circular door of the vault, in a great ring of glimmering steel, shines like an immense jewel set in dull silver. This door, as lovely and intricate as the works of a watch, is lit up at night by reflected lighting, and people halt on the pavement to peer in and wonder where that lunar-like illumination comes from. A rumour even went about that the door was made of solid silver. All this sort of thing, need we add, is Good Business. Get people wondering, and they'll talk; and talk is the material of prosperity, humanity being what it is.

I should not have paused so long over this bank if it did not beautifully illustrate the point I am clumsily trying to sharpen. The people who work in the Equitable Trust Company of Atlantic City, when they moved into their new building, suddenly found themselves, unexpectedly, amazingly, and by the genius of the architect who had planned and executed their new quarters, living daily among surroundings of beauty. And lo, how they responded, as people almost always will. Their own pride was involved. We asked one of the janitors what he thought about the building. "I'd like to see any one scratch it!" he replied, almost fiercely. The woman who comes in to cook lunch for

the staff in their pretty dining room upstairs hastened
to show off to Titania her icebox and ice-making machine which was turning out delicious little transparent
cubes. Mr. Kelly, the cashier, related how at board
meetings an unwary director who began to tilt back
on the hind legs of his chair, as he had always done in
the old building, was instantly called to order by his
fellows. "Here, you can't do that *now!*" And yet
these were the same old severe office armchairs they had
always used—but the ingenious architect had scraped
off the ugly old mahogany colour and repainted them
deliciously in blue and green and little innocent gaieties
of colour. And now Mr. Kelly himself, though he
wants to put a filing case by his desk, does not dare do
so until he has consulted the architect. He is fearful
of doing something that won't harmonize with his
gracious surroundings. There isn't a thing in the whole
building, from lighting fixtures to radiator screens,
from window curtains to the racks for deposit slips,
that isn't a perfectly planned integral in a harmonious
whole, as prettily thought out as a boudoir of Old
France. The place is bright and strong and charming
as a jewel casket. That is what one means by the
spirit of Art. It is a sense of pride in the thing itself,
over and above its mere utility.

So we returned to the hotel, and ordered shish kebab.
This, as we had been accustomed to it, was merely little
gobbets of lamb on a skewer, surrounded by sierras of
rice. But these kebabs were divided one from other
by small segments of red pepper; and then, nestling between each morsel of meat and the pepper, what do you

suppose we found? A leaf of mint. There it was again, the memorandum of art. It was the little, unnecessary wizard's touch—like the tonka bean in the tobacco that pervades and promotes the whole. I said to Titania: "I'm going to write a piece about the tonka bean as an emblem of the artistic spirit."

THE MIDDLE COUNTRY ROAD

ONCE I collaborated in writing a novel. In fact, twice; but the first seizure was never read by any one. In the second case it was my partner who planned that the scene should be laid at the eastern end of Long Island; but when the time came for writing that part of the story my colleague had gone abroad. I gave a quite circumstantial description of the extremities of Paumanok; which was meritorious, as I had never seen them. I have often wondered whether my collaborator, whom I will conceal under the name of D—— M——, has ever been there himself. I concealed my ignorance from him; perhaps he his from me.

This is only the preamble. The amble itself is that the other day it occurred to me that it would be an honest thing to find out whether that part of Long

The Romany Stain

Island is at all like my description of it. Besides, a new car is a great incentive to travel. So Titania and I got into Dean Swift and went eastward.

I foresee that I am not going to be able to tell you as much as I should like to about the scenery. There are always so many agreeable analogies that flit into the mind and impede narration. In the case of the novel that D—— M—— and I wrote we ruled out all philosophizing; the narrative (if I do have to say it, because the publisher never did) was delightfully rapid. This was because the story was written with the firm intention of selling it to the movies; which has not yet been consummated. The agent complained that it did not have enough Lust at First Sight. He said (he is a well-read man, the agent) that it was neither one Dell nor the other: neither Floyd nor Ethel. He said there was no Pola Negri in our woodpile. If I had the clipping here I believe I would tell you what the New York *Times* said about that story. Why, it was a perfectly splendid notice. If you will turn back to your file of the *Times*, May 25, 1924, you can see. Another reason why the story moved so swiftly was that both D—— M—— and I had determined we would create the most delightful girl in modern fiction; then we both fell in love with her and wanted to write all the bits of dialogue belonging to her; so each one hastened on and on, to get past his allotted section and into the other man's. That was why it only took two and a half years to write the book. The real reason was that we had drawn some advance money from the publisher on the strength of the mere synopsis. Nothing makes a

book so hard to write as having got money for it beforehand. Let this be a warning to publishers.

But, as I began to say, Titania and I set off eastward. The reason why I shall not say much about the
scenery is that I didn't really study it in detail. I got
the *feeling* of it rather than any precise observation.
For driving a new car is a gloriously introspective business. You are too happy listening to the unfamiliar
drum of the engine, watching the strange dashboard,
learning her ways (I may as well tell you that seven
notches below the bead seems to be the best adjustment
for the carburetor intake-screw in the case of Dean
Swift) to carefully examine the landscape or worry
about split infinitives. Then, too, you have a clock on
the dashboard, which is a new luxury in my motoring
career; it is an eight-day clock, and you may get to
thinking, suppose you wind an eight-day clock every
Sunday, then once every eight weeks (wouldn't it be?)
you should let her go a week without winding, to work
off the excess torsion? Titania and I stopped the Dean
in a pine wood along the Middle Country Road to argue
that out. Driving a new car is very like being young,
which is only driving a new mind and body through
life. You are likely to be so eagerly absorbed in your
own mechanisms that you don't really pay proper attention to the meaning of what is around you. All
the time you have the feeling, some day I'll do this
again, thoughtfully, and study the significance of it.
But suppose you aren't going to have any chance to do
it again?

So I had better tell you at once how lovely is the

Middle Country Road. The general human habit of keeping to the main highway is a great consolation to those who always hunt out the roads marked second-rate in the maps. So when everyone else, at the romantic hamlet of Smithtown Branch, bears left on the concrete pike to Port Jeff, the Dean (whose garage, by the way, is called the Deanery; and if you're disturbed by the idea of a female Dean you need only think of Bryn Mawr College) the Dean keeps straight on into the strange and barren peace of the Middle Country. I think it is there (the map is not handy as I write) that you reach the hamlet of Coram; but it is not Coram Populo, for all that region is rather desolate. What beautiful little old farmhouses, deserted and crumbling by the way, where lilacs still in the dooryard bloom. And queer, tiny forgotten cemeteries; in one of these a waggon and two white horses were standing; Titania said (I was looking at the oil gauge just then) they were digging up the graves. She remembered the white horses of Rosmersholm. I like to spell it waggon, because (this is the Urchin's pun) every waggon ought to have a geegee.

There was something curiously metaphysical about our little voyage. First the Friends' Meeting House at Jericho. Then West Hills, where Walt was born. Then, as I am telling you, the exquisitely forlorn quality of the Middle Country Road (*medio tutissimus ibis*). At sunset time you come into Riverhead where the friendly and humorous proprietor of the old Griffin House makes you welcome. In the hotel you will find a facsimile of what purports to be a liquor license once issued to Abraham Lincoln. In the dining room Mary the waitress, with an excellent Long Island twang, announces suddenly over your shoulder, "We have steak, lamb chops, veal cutlet, fried clams, fried eels." And in the pine woods along the bay, at dusk, the whippoorwills are shrilling, like a flexible switch flogged in air.

D—— M—— and I were quite safe in describing the island of our story, because it is private property anyway and small chance of any one checking us up. But the other island in that bay, Shelter Island, is very much as I had imagined it and certainly an enchanting place. The cheerful young ferryman at the South Ferry on Shelter Island had been on the island of our story, and told me of its charms, of its woods full of deer and its steep clay cliffs. He is a student of thunderstorms, too, and told how the tides alter the behaviour of electrical storms in that narrow gut; and how a young farmer in the neighbourhood was killed by lightning recently while taking a bath in a galvanized tub under an electric light fixture.

But the real goal of our pilgrimage was Montauk, which was as surprising to me as almost everything is when you see it for yourself. As far as Amagansett the South Shore highway, superb of its kind, is almost distressingly point-device. The Hamptons are all ye'd up: even Uncle Sam lends his approval: I could hardly believe the inscription *Ye Easthampton Post Office*. At Southampton I think my eye caught a sign on Agawam Pond about Not Luring The Swans. That would bar out Leda. The delightful windmills of the Hamptons have mostly lost their sails: perhaps someone has been tilting at them.

But beyond Amagansett the Dean found herself, in a gathering fog, on a queer undulating way among wild sand dunes and heathy moors. For many miles that strange road twists and thankyoumaams in the desert. Under the cliffs the surf roared in dim vagues of milk and pearl; and when at last we reached the lighthouse and shut off the motor a savage lonely voice came bursting through the fog. It was the siren; an odd name for such a melancholy warning cry. One could not help remembering it was here, along these lonely beaches, that Walt Whitman used to shout Shakespeare at the storm.

Coming home next morning, in the clear sunlight of the Shinnecock Hills, just as we were approaching a big truck, I saw—too late to do anything—a fine big yellow and black turtle crawling out on to the road. I'm afraid that he was going exactly into the path of those great flat wheels. And another omen led me to fear the worst had happened. That afternoon we were spinning gently along the Motor Parkway; which, as the signs remind you, is reserved for Pleasure Vehicles. Behind us came a roaring, a car shot past the Dean at twice our speed. It was a hearse.

THE CONSTANT NYMPH

BEFORE me is a newspaper photograph of her; great ropes taut round her waist and under her armpits; lashed to the wrecking company's derrick like the skipper's daughter on the *Hesperus*, or Andromeda on her rocky jut. She is coming down to-day; and New York University is the only Perseus who has volunteered to rescue this Constant Nymph.

The day Diana came down from the tower of Madison Square Garden something went away from New York. It is foolish to grumble about saying good-bye to anything we love. The Technique of Saying Good-bye is one of the great unwritten poems. But for me she will always leave, like Mr. Markham's cedar tree, a lonesome place against the sky.

The day Diana came down all continued in its usual course. In the slack morning hours people were riding

[251]

in the subway, picking up jettisoned newspapers to pass away the time. The *Berengaria* turned her great nose toward sea. Editors were busy sending back MSS., with courteous letters explaining why the poems were unavailable. One of these editors happened to tell me that he was stiff all over from a day spent in his garden, planting laurel. (Planting laurel! Exactly what an editor should be doing, I thought.) Six-cylinder cars were making that magnificent rich droning hum as they shifted into second speed. (Only a man who is just driving six-cylinders for the first time knows how splendid that sound is. Yes: Dame Quickly has a younger sister: her name is Dean Swift. The new Everyman edition of the "Journal to Stella" is carried in one of her door pockets as a talisman. We hitch our wagon to Stella.) Between the acts of great plays—such as "Rosmersholm"—people talked busily to avert the painful impact of thought. In the Thirty-fourth Street region gross terraces of building stood magnificently in soft blue air. A new anthology of poems was published—Burton Stevenson's "Home Book of Modern Verse." A book so fascinating that in spite of its eleven hundred pages I could not resist toting it around with me all day, to read on the train and in the subway. For, absurdly enough, I felt that the publication of that book was the consolation, the counterpoise, to Diana's come-down. Eros is gone from Piccadilly Circus, Diana is gone from Madison Square, but at least in poetry books the gods still live. No one shall rip them the black spot.

The day Diana came down something went away

from New York. I don't know just what; no one can say. Whatever it was, it could only be suggested in verse. A friend of mine told me that he is taking singing lessons, because, he said, You can say so many things in singing that you couldn't possibly utter in ordinary speech. There never was a truer word. In an anthology like Mr. Stevenson's (a codicil to his fat and famous "Home Book of Verse") you can find out what people are really thinking about. The world has long since agreed that in poetry you may say what you mean; no one is offended at poetry. It is only in prose that you must be wary. It is like the old saying (Joseph Conrad makes a splendidly urbane reference to it somewhere) about one man being able to steal a horse without scandal, whereas another may not even look wistfully at a halter. But it is true (Conrad adds) that some people have a particularly irritating way of gazing at halters. This is true also in the stable of the horse called Pegasus.

The day Diana came down something went away. I suppose that some day I may see her again at New York University, but I would almost rather not. For me she must always live in that particular eddy of sky that hangs above Madison Square. When it has to be done, I can say good-bye with the rest of them. But there's no law against my thinking of the old house on Madison Avenue (gone also) where three young men once lived with causeless merriment and regarded Diana as their patron deity. They would be as chaste and lofty as herself; offensive to their decent minds were the rumours of stag parties associated with the goddess.

The Romany Stain

What did she mean to them? Who could say? Perhaps they felt, dumbly, that scheme life as you will, intersperse it with jocular palaver and consoling hurry, there remains above all the fierce principle of beauty, the untamed goddess of the hunt, pursuing the wild animals of desire with her sharp arrow of reason. And yet she never shoots her arrow. Ah, how that bothered those meditative young men! And a later generation of bipeds, the balloon-trousered squires of N. Y. U., will probably brood the same awkward analogue. What, meanwhile, has become of the winged mischief of Piccadilly Circus? As I remember him he was not aiming a never-to-be-shot-off dart. He was skipping on the very tiptoe of exultant malice: he had actually sped the shaft. As Eros, of course, would have; everyone knows how much more hasty they are on the incontinent of Europe. One could imagine the prickling wand transpiercing someone in that throng; yes, even some hale and fresh-bathed Briton, in silk hat and morning coat, trembling with that naughty fixture in his breast. Or better still: some docile young American, hastening through the Circus, who suddenly found the daintily feathered shaft stuck right through him. How he implored the door-man at the Trocadero to pull it out, and the latter thought him surprisingly tight for so early in the afternoon. How he dodged zigzag through the crowd, to avoid poking his awkward skewer into other people. My advice to that young man would be to hurry to George Santayana and beg him to pluck it out.—Or suppose this had happened to Henry James? Perhaps that is exactly what *did* happen to Henry James; he had to stand off a bit from the world lest people should see his arrow.—I must look up the legend of St. Sebastian.

The day Diana came down something went away from New York. Some little shuddering pang of loveliness and loneliness, something that I hear sometimes between the strident jangles of a street-organ tune or in the voices of ships in the river. Perhaps I'm glad they've taken her away; it is good to have beautiful things near you for a while, and then lose them, for only so (I suppose) can you be properly disciplined. Only so (again, perhaps) can you remember that men write poetry for other reasons than because *dust* rhymes with *thrust* and *star* with *far*. The day she went away things went on much as usual. The traffic beacons twinkled in unison up and down Fifth Avenue, the great tide of cars (six-cylinders) carried "women of the better class" (see Oliver Herford's gorgeous poem, p. 537 of Burton Stevenson's anthology) about their delightful mundanities, Congreve and Ibsen taught contemporary playwrights that neither lust nor chastity were entirely post-war inventions. No more shall I see her distant grace against heaven, tightening her arrow toward a rising moon, threatening our thick air with her gay pagan archery. Perhaps, near at hand, she was not beautiful at all.

Since writing the above I have walked up Fourth Avenue and seen her with the workmen round her, about to lower her from the skeleton remnant of her tower. Madison Square was black with Actæons. I dare say they were making ribald jokes; but worse than that a Life Insurance Company had attached its initialed house flag to her. I was glad O. Henry, who loved her, was not there to see. Yet there are always various interpretations. Perhaps the life insurers intended the flag to drape round her and shield her as she descended. But I can't help thinking that her sister of Ephesus had the more glorious fate. I wished there had been some Zoning Law to forbid those great ropes so tight about her lovely waist.

The day Diana came down something went away from New York. There was no multitude all with one voice crying out Great is Diana of the Manhattans. But the arrow she never shot sticks in my heart.

CHRISTMAS CARDBOARD

I HAVE no idea who are the happy manufacturers of those sheets of coloured cardboard; but when they book their reorders early in January they must notice, in the region of western Long Island, a pleasant depletion of stock among the village stationers. This means that the Urchin and I have begun the winter season of Cut-Outs.

It is a very simple pleasure; only requiring plenty of cardboard of different colours, scissors, and paste. To these may be added silver foil (such as comes as inner wrappings in tobacco packages), tissue paper of various colours, even paper clips (stolen from the office): if you are very luxurious, a box of water colours. But the cardboard and scissors and paste are the essentials. No Postexpressionist in a German *Schauspielhaus*, no imaginative Czechoslovak director or Viennese experimenter in *Andeutungstechnik* has more fun

than the Urchin and I with our cardboard stage sets.
I read in the *Theatre Arts Monthly* of the "frenetic
ardour of Klein's décors"; I read that

a delirious period of representational renunciation set
in, in which all form was eliminated save the form of
disembodied passion. . . . Artistic unity as well
as the foreign exchange compelled an austere simplicity
bordering on nudity. . . . Jessner is a disciple of
the Reinhardt Theatre, remoulded in the womb of the
expressionistic era. He retains a measure of structural
verisimilitude in his sets. . . . He conceives the
word and the scene equally in terms of massed levels
rising harmoniously to a dramatic resolution.

I read these things, and I realize, of course, that the
Urchin and I have no chance of being taken seriously
as stage designers until we learn to exhale a lingo like
that. But I wonder, a little timidly, why it is that men
feel it necessary to take the most fascinating and childlike of all games—the game of the theatre—and wrap
it up in such ponderous technical talk. I should like
to have heard Will Shakespeare and Ben Jonson dis-
cussing the problem of stage sets. And (to tell you
the truth) I am getting a little weary of the word
"plastic." I read again in the *Theatre Arts Monthly*,
a fascinating magazine but terribly bullied by the
current jargon of the *Andeutungsbuehne*, that

The modern German theatre, from the flat motionless
surface of the backdrop to the animate, plastic form of
the actor moving in space, is creating an intermediate

form, holding in its rhythmic lines the elements of rest and motion in one.

Surely we might have taken for granted (Ben Jonson would say?) that the backdrop is a background and the actor is "plastic." We believe so fully and enthusiastically in the things the modern theatre is trying to work out that we hate to see those things too fogged up with jargon.

Anyhow, the Urchin and I take all those matters for granted. He knows, wise elf, that what we are trying to work out is merely something that will please the eye and convey some sense of reality as simply and colourfully as possible. It may be our set of Queenstown Harbour at twilight, for instance. In the foreground a rough promontory, profiled out of green cardboard, is surmounted by a white lighthouse. A thin, undulated strip of blue cardboard represents a gentle agitation of the Atlantic. ("Elements of rest and motion in one.") Then, cunningly arranged on a slant, so that she appears to be moving toward us out of the land-locked bay, is the silhouette of a fine steamship, cut out of black card. Small rows of perforations serve for ports, and a toy flashlight laid behind her gives them a pleasant sparkle. And, backdrop for the whole, is one large sheet of blue, against which is pasted (in green) an outline of low Irish hills. Six silhouettes in all, cut out of different coloured sheets of card, are the total equipment. We challenge you to say it isn't an excellent sight, when decently propped up with little cardboard easels behind the flats. You can even, if you are feeling excessive, insert a declining sun (of

orange cardboard) just slipping into a notch of the
Celtic landscape. Fine enough! And the Urchin goes
to bed in an ecstasy.

There was a snow scene that we set great store by.
It represented (if we must tell the truth) the rustic
home of an animal known in our family as "Mr. Gissing." The house, built up of white cardboard, was
set upon a large white expanse representing heavy snow-
fall—drifts may be piled up with cotton wool, where
the arduous Mr. Gissing has shovelled clear his small
brick path (a strip of red cardboard). You have no
idea what excellent icicles, festooned along the eaves,
can be serrated out of silver foil. Sombre pine trees,
cut of green cardboard, stand behind the house. Between two of the trunks stretches a thread, on which
hang (cut out of white notepaper) some garments
belonging to Mr. Gissing's puppies. Over the windows
you paste red tissue paper; and against this tissue paper,
on the inside, are affixed silhouettes of the puppies
themselves, looking eagerly out (tongues excitedly de-
pending) for the arrival of Santa Claus. The house
is illuminated within by the same small flashlight
which served a few minutes ago for the portholes of
the *Mauretania*. (The more funnels a ship has the
better for the scene.) The European *régisseurs* touch
on a painful point when they speak of "representational
renunciation." The Urchin and I have had to renounce a good many tempting effects because our
régisseur will have supper served along toward seven
o'clock. And the dining table is really the best place
for getting fine rhythms and tempos. The chandelier is

Christmas Cardboard

handy for complex lighting devices, such as are needed by a black background of sky with a careful pattern of the Dipper pricked in, light shining through it from behind.

When you get into the matter of interiors, all is more difficult. That's what we're working on now. Like Mr. Bel-Geddes, the Urchin and I are very keen for long flights of steps; but they are devilish things to cut out of cardboard and fold up and paste together in a stable congruity. Then, when you start tinkering with oblique perspectives—such as a wide doorway lit from behind (the flashlight again; we'll have to have more than one flashlight pretty soon), with a flight of stairs coming down at an angle and a little mirror on the wall near Mr. Gissing's hatrack (silver paper makes a fine mirror), you can see that we are up against Real Stuff. Another problem: the cardboard manufacturers have been rather shabby in their blue sheets. The blue isn't a clear, bright, lively tint; it is rather leaden and sour. That makes it hard to get just the effect of a lucent Christmas Eve sky, which was what we desiderated behind those tall French windows at the rear of the set. We shall have to play quite a violent jet of toy flashlight illumination upon that blue cardboard to tone it up to the proper luminosity.

I rather meant to tell you about the model of a tugboat that we have devised. But I want to catch the 5:09 train. The Urchin is waiting for another go at that oblique staircase. And it's a point of honour with us not to work independently. It's like Beaumont and Fletcher: when the job is done, we hardly know which has done what.

ROUND COLUMBUS CIRCLE

[March, 1923]

THE other evening as I was walking along Fifty-ninth Street I noticed a man buying a copy of *Variety* at a newsstand. Obedient to my theory that life deserves all possible scrutiny, I thought it would be interesting to follow him and see exactly what he did.

I chose my quarry not merely at random. People who read *Variety* are likely to be interesting because they are pretty sure to be connected, no matter how remotely, with that odd, unpredictable, and high-spirited race who call themselves "artists," or "professionals." He might be in vaudeville, or in burlesque, or in the world of "outdoor shows." He might be a "carnival man," or a cabaret performer, a dancer, an "equilibrist," a marimba bandsman, a "sensational perch artist," a "lightning change artist," a "jass baby," a saxophonist. He might be the manager of a picture house; he might be in the legitimate. He might even be one of my favourite pair of artists (of whom I think with affection: I have never seen them, but their professional card appears now and then in *Variety*— "Null and Void, The Dippy Daffy Duo").

So I followed him discreetly, to see what might happen.

At Columbus Circle he paused and looked about him rather as though he felt himself in a congenial element. The blue mildness of the night was bright with exciting signs, the ancient one of the full moon seeming rather pallid compared to the electric picture of Socony Oil pouring from a can into a funnel. There was a constant curving flow of skittering taxis, especially the kind that have slatted black panels abaft the windows: these look like little closed shutters and give a sense of secrecy, mystery, and vivid romance. Upon all this my fugitive gazed with a sort of affection; then he turned and stood a minute before the window of Childs' where small gas flames were as blue as violets under the griddle. I supposed that perhaps he was hungry, for he gazed pensively; but perhaps he was also thinking that the restaurant had quaintly changed its sex since afternoon; for now it was bustling with white-clad men instead of the laundered ladies of a few hours ago. He went on to an adjoining florist's window, and here he studied the lilacs, orchids (in their little individual test tubes), lilies of the valley, forsythia, narcissus, daffodils, pussy-willows, sweet peas. It was a very springlike window. I saw his eye fall upon the deftly wrapped sheaves of paper inside the shop, where bright colours glimmered through swathes of pale green tissue. These parcels were all addressed; ready to go out, I supposed, to very beautiful ladies.

He passed on (he had lit a pipe, by the way) by the Park Theatre, and he cast an observant eye upon that, noting that it was dark. Perhaps he pondered the vicissitudes of the show business. The windows of several haberdashers, all announcing their proximate retirement from traffic, won declensions from his eye: there were some quite lively shirts at $1.85 that seemed nearly to obtain his suffrage. But again I saw him lured by food. A very minute, narrow doggery, intensely masculine in aspect, but with its courteous legend LADIES INVITED glossed upon the pane, exhibited a tray of hamburger steak, liberally besprinkled with onion slivers. These he gravely considered. But still he proceeded; and still, in the phrase of Mr. Montague, I "committed myself to his vestiges."

It was the automobile business, next, that drew his attention. Those astonishing windows just south of the Circle plainly afforded him material for thought —places where, in great halls of baronial aspect, on Oriental rugs and marble floors, under little whispering galleries where the salesmen retire to their orisons, America's most shining triumphs are displayed. He was fascinated by the window of U. S. Rubber—where a single tire, mounted on a canary-coloured wheel, and an array of galoshes and arctics, are gravely displayed under tall blue hangings and festoons of artificial flowers. Or the Goodrich window, where a huge flattened circlet has the space to itself on a crinkled wealth of purple-green shot silk. Amethystine lights shine through glazed screens behind this monstrous tire: drapes of imitation Spanish moss and enormous vases give the effect of a vaudeville stage set for some juggling act. The automobile business has learned all the tricks of Victorian stage *decor;* perhaps that was why my *Variety* reader was so thrilled. Another window, where the car comes bravely to the aid of the hard-pressed Church ("To Church in Their Chevrolet"—have you seen it?), is even more dramatic. Here the department store lends a hand also, for the modes worn by the figures are from Fifth Avenue. I was rather thrilled when I saw my fugitive halt also in front of the Dame Quickly showroom: a much more businesslike display, where the latest models of the Quickly family exhibit their modest and competent elegance.

But it was most interesting of all to find him striking off Broadway and entering the lobby of the Grenoble Hotel. He peered about the lobby as though he were expecting to meet someone; but I couldn't help suspecting that this was chiefly for the benefit of the clerk at the desk; what he really wanted was a quiet place to sit down and read his *Variety*. At any rate, he occupied the resilient corner of a couch for some time, studiously conning the magazine. I should have liked to tell the clerk behind the counter the reason why the Grenoble is always a special place to me—it was there, I believe, that Rudyard Kipling lay dangerously ill twenty-five years ago. I wonder if the hotel register holds any record of that momentous incident.

The Romany Stain

Presently—after carefully scanning the columns which tell how much each play took in at the box-office last week: perhaps the only positively accurate gauge of New York theatrical tastes; you will learn with surprise, for instance, that one of the leading moneymakers is a show called "Abie's Irish Rose"—my subject folded up *Variety* and set forth again. Following, I was pleased to see him stop at Mr. Keyte's bookshop on Fifty-seventh Street; and even more surprised to note that the thing that seemed most to catch his eye was a fine photo of Henry James. He complimented the sales-lady upon it, and he bought a book. It was a copy of Sherwood Anderson's *Winesburg, Ohio*, in the "Modern Library."

But it was plain that all this time the idea of food had been loitering agreeably in the back of his mind. I trailed him back to Columbus Circle, and there, to my amusement, he returned straight to the little hash-alley where he had admired the meat patties with onions. He went in and sat down at the tiny counter. "Hamburg steak," he said, "and put plenty of onions on it." And then, after a moment, "Coffee with plenty," he added.

"It's plenty of everything with you to-night," said the whitecoat, genially.

"Sure, everything but money," remarked this mysterious creature. He propped up his *Winesburg* against the sugar basin and read while he ate.

At this point, fearing that my sleuthing might cause him to become self-conscious, I went thoughtfully away.

A SEPARATION

I HAVEN'T seen her for four days. Not since she spent her first night (in a manner of speaking) away from home. . . . This, by the way, is for parents only. Others won't understand.

Babblings, as I call her when we are alone, is eight months old. As you know, about that age these minuscule creatures are likely to be turned over to the care of a nurse. Well, now, *how* can I put it delicately? These outspoken medical fellows would simply say she had been weaned and leave it at that. The point is that the small creature sleeps in the nursery, and no longer in the bedroom with her parents. And so if you run for town early in the morning and don't get back at night until after dark, when will you see her? Not at all, until the week end.

The Romany Stain

I haven't seen her for four days: and walking home the other evening I realized what I had been missing. Why, her, the absurd microcosm. That little yammer, or (let's be honest) that sudden rousing squall, beginning in the middlenight as suddenly as a locomotive blows off steam; ending with equal suddenness when a familiar form leaned over the crib; those queer rhythmical whimpers of cheer when, completely pleased, she was pushing herself down the psychic slopes of sleep; the excitement when she first rolled over, raised her head like a turtle, and gazed about with an air of triumph (until she learned that, also like the slug testudo, she couldn't get back) . . . these were what I lacked.

I *said* you wouldn't understand, didn't I?

But what I missed most of all were those private conferences we had, before breakfast, while I was getting dressed. The rest of the family being already at table, and cries coming aloft ("You'll miss your train"), what was I doing? Well, that was the time when I was calling her . . . I told you what I called her. We were alone. As I was tying my tie, she could watch me from the crib. I don't know just what she was laughing at. But anyhow, and since I'm not going to go into details, we had a few brief merriments together. We both understood them perfectly, each in our own way. She won't tell about them—no, not ever—because she won't remember them: and I am not one to let loose secrets shared with a lady, even the youngest. No, we'll respect an eternity of taciturnity. I'll have to confess, however, that there was just a little element of trickery on my part. Because, dressing finished, tie tied, hair brushed, all ready to make a break for the cup of coffee and the train, I wasn't quite honest. I gave her a kinsprit grin, and said (this was pretty bad): "I'll be right back." I think she got the impression I was just going out of the room for a moment or so and would return to be entertained further. In that way I got off without distressing her. And then I never did come back, not till night time. It wasn't quite straight, maybe. I remember that her eyes followed me to the door.

This is bad; because I'm giving the impression that she liked me as much as I liked her. That's not so, of course. In a few seconds she had forgotten me entirely. She had far better company, all day long. The best company in the world, indeed. And of course I had plenty to think about, myself. But I didn't realize, until the bedroom was so painfully quiet, how much she meant. . . . And I haven't *seen* her for four days, not since she spent her first night away from home, in a manner of speaking.

THE UNWRITTEN BOOK

MANY critics have spoken—and many more will speak—of Doughty's "Arabia" as one of the world's great travel books. What they have said is true; though we doubt if that terrible, exhausting, and fiery work will ever be popular, though it may readily become fashionable.

But there is a book of travel (or travail) still to be written, dealing with a wilderness even more appalling than the Arabian desert, a book that might possibly be just as great as—or greater than—Doughty's. That is the book, unwritable perhaps, that would deal adequately, honestly, with the terrible, magnificent jungle of New York. Perhaps desert is a better word for it than jungle, for in a desert the sand leaves no trace of your passage. But I stick to the idea of a jungle, for it has strange and fantastic analogies. Through these vast thickets, trudging elate or despairing, each explorer beats out his own little paths of precarious safety. Lie covert near where the spiritual tracks cross one another—in a newspaper office, for example, a bewildering ganglion of threaded human nerves and passions—and watch the inhabitants of the forest padding softly on their strange quests. For, like the wild animals, each has his own secret, instinctive way toward some Drinking Place. Or you may stand, if you prefer, dumbly contemplating the pitiful bright-ness of the steel-plated subway stairs—brightness worn by millions of tragic, hopeful feet.

Like aisles of darkness under the dense tropic foliage are those subway tunnels, green and red lights brilliant as parrakeets in the gloom. Bright as clumps of poisonous orchids are the little news-kennels with their coloured magazine covers. Poison, poison to the spirit, the thoughtful explorer may mutter to himself, and stoutly avert the eye. At every turning in the jungle, beside every thicket, or under the huge spreading palm-tree girders of the Pennsylvania trainshed, he may imagine he hears the sudden soft whir of Time's savage arrow, feathered so prettily, flicked into the body of some fellow traveller. The shrill call of the traffic cop's whistle, is it not dreadfully like the cry of some threat-ening parrot or macaw, perched ironically above the throng? That cry halts even the great pachyderms and the chattering monkeys, all on their way to some Drinking Place of their own. Like a huge yellow py-thon you can see the L train winding among the tall bamboo groves of buildings. And you must struggle with everyone, even with your own indolent soul, for command of your spirit in that monstrous jungle.

The analogies are terrible indeed! In that frenzy of haste and friendliness, where the traveller must even struggle against his well-loved comrades for the endangered command of his own soul; where silly half-truths are so fashionable and so well rewarded that even the desire to write honourable candour easily grows dim; where sometimes one almost attains the ultimate and most fearful disillusion—that God Himself is in a hurry; in that jungle be wary and be calm, my soul. The whole jungle conspires and rustles with menace; it is thick with beauty and terror; how swiftly the creepers wind you in if you try to pause for reason and peace. Strange enemies, in the loveliest of sleek stripings, lie on the branching limbs overhead, waiting to spring; crouch in the long grass, eager to strike. In that jungle men cannot even worship God without quarrelling about it. The strangest laughters are heard, sounding through the stillness; the lapping of the thirsty creatures is anxiously suspended as they raise their heads and listen to the queer voices of the night.

Magnificent, thrilling, inexplicable wilderness! Chop through it your own little paths, endangered soul; find your own strange hidden waters of refreshment. And pay no need to any wisdom save your own. There are the quaintest flutings and voices of decoy. The owl has a beguiling murmur; the adder a shining skin. Be childish in your sullen wisdom, O wandering spirit! It is of this wilderness that some day a book might be

The Unwritten Book

written. Yet perhaps it has been written already—the greatest book of our time, maybe, if your mind runs that way. You can always tell when a book is really great—does it become a classic for children? For men, terribly fearing the sharp wisdom of fables, always soften them by pretending they were written for children. It happened to Swift, for instance. And the greatest book of our time, perhaps, is "The Jungle Book."

Magnificent, terrible jungle of New York! Like Mowgli, you must learn to run with the wolves, and learn to love them, for they are lovable and brave. But be wary, O soul; for there will come a time when you must return to live with men.

THE END